Helen Fielding's
Bridget Jones's Diary

CONTINUUM CONTEMPORARIES

Also available in this series

Forthcoming in this series:

· HELEN FIELDING'S

Bridget Jones's Diary

A READER'S GUIDE

IMELDA WHELEHAN

CONTINUUM | NEW YORK | LONDON

2002

The Continuum International Publishing Group Inc
370 Lexington Avenue, New York, NY 10017

The Continuum International Publishing Group Ltd
The Tower Building, 11 York Road, London SE1 7NX

www.continuumbooks.com

Printed in the United States of America

Library of Congress Cataloging-in-Publication Data

Whelehan, Imelda, 1960–
    Helen Fielding's Bridget Jones's diary : a reader's guide / Imelda
Whelehan.
        p. cm. — (Continuum contemporaries)
    Includes bibliographical references.
    ISBN 0-8264-5322-8 (alk. paper)
    1. Fielding, Helen, 1958– Bridget Jones's diary. 2. London
(England)—In literature. 3. Single women in literature. I. Fielding,
Helen, 1958– Bridget Jones's diary. II. Title. III. Series.
    PR6056.I4588 B7539 2002
    823'.914—dc21
                                            2002000885
ISBN 0-8264-5322-8

Contents

For Lucilla Zanetti
A diarist in her youth.

Acknowledgements

Heartfelt thanks to Kathleen Bell and Dennis Cheetham for helpful conversations and unfailingly acute observations on *Bridget Jones's Diary*. Thanks also to David, Miriam and Laurence Sadler.

1

The Novelist

Born in 1959, Helen Fielding is the daughter of a mill manager, and comes from Morley, West Yorkshire. She read English at St. Anne's College, Oxford University, graduating in 1979. After this, she won a BBC traineeship and worked there for 10 years on various programs, later working on a series of films in Ethiopia, Sudan, and Mozambique for Comic Relief—the charity set up by television comedy stars and resulting in regular campaigns ever since. Fielding had early aspirations as a writer and attempted a romance novel which was apparently summarily rejected by Mills & Boon. Her experiences with Comic Relief and filming the famine relief attempts in Africa are fictionalized in her first novel, *Cause Celeb* (1994). Its heroine, Rosie Richardson, becomes an aid worker, having previously worked as a publicist for a London publisher, where she met and fell in love with arts program presenter Oliver Marchant.

After her time at the BBC, Fielding became a freelance journalist, writing features and food reviews, but she became more widely known once the identity of the author of the column "Bridget Jones's Diary" was revealed. The column first appeared in the

Independent on February 28, 1995, and, according to then features editor Charles Leadbeater, it derived its impetus from columns like Dulcie Domum's diary (in the *Guardian*), but with a target group of younger women. For Leadbeater, Fielding was regarded as an ideal writer of such a column on the basis of *Cause Celeb*, which has a similarly hapless, but more feisty first-person narrator. The wider success he puts down entirely to Helen Fielding's considerable talent. The columns carried a by-line photograph, actually of Susannah Lewis, a secretary at the *Independent* newspaper, holding a cigarette and a wine glass, which seemed to contribute to the notion that Bridget actually existed, and resulted in fan mail and marriage proposals. The column was later to move to the *Telegraph* in 1997.

Helen Fielding asserts that Bridget Jones is based on a character she once tried to write into a sitcom about a single girl; the diary format was apparently inspired by her looking back at her own calorie-obsessed diaries, produced during her college years. Both readers and critics alike have been keen to know whether Fielding drew on her own experiences to create Bridget—and perhaps the diary format makes these kinds of questions and comparisons inevitable. While Fielding consistently denies that Bridget is meant to be her, she concedes that two of her close friends, Tracey McLeod, a TV presenter, and Sharon Maguire, a TV director, were the models for Jude and Shazzer in the novel. Later, Fielding would lobby for Sharon Maguire to direct the film version of *Bridget Jones* and this would become Maguire's film debut. Maguire acknowledges that she is the inspiration for Shazzer, and did indeed coin the term "emotional fuckwit," as well as being prone to the odd drunken rant about the men in her life. She affirms that the life of Bridget and her friends in some sense draws on the escapades of Helen Fielding, Tracey MacLeod, and herself in the early 1990s; but, importantly for the success of the novel, Bridget is a kind of "everywoman" of the 1990s.

Bridget's life, aspirations, and consumer tastes to a large extent reflect the tastes, trends, and popular cultural milieux of glossy women's magazines and popular television in the mid 1990s, and this is what makes her so instantly recognizable to so many readers who have the same cultural diet. What is more surprising is that even though the book directly appealed to women in their mid-twenties to early forties, it also gained fans in men and women of all ages. One famous male admirer, whose assurance that "even men will laugh" appears on the cover of the UK paperback, is Salman Rushdie, who later made a guest appearance in the film. Even in the United States, where many of the individual references might baffle the average reader, people recognized a type of person close enough to their own experiences, or experiences they were used to seeing represented in sitcoms and the popular press, for Bridget to strike a chord with them.

Fielding had agreed to write the Bridget Jones column in order to support herself while writing her second novel (which, she says, "was rather earnest and about the Caribbean"), so it is ironic that this column would itself provide the raw material for what would actually become her second novel, *Bridget Jones's Diary*. Much of the material and incident from the columns would survive virtually intact in the novel—the first column, for instance, features Bridget on "permanent date-with-Daniel standby," and an example of one of their email exchanges. Some of the more topical references in the columns—for example to the UK traffic cones hotline—had been removed by the time the novel was devised, and whereas a weekly column could afford to be episodic, the novel would need a clearer structure to hold it together. Perhaps one of the attractions of the diary format is that it provides a natural structure which Fielding strengthens by having a classic romance plot thread its way through the novel.

Bridget Jones's Diary, published in hardback in the UK in 1996 and in the United States in 1998, has since been translated into at least 33 languages. This success brought almost overnight celebrity status to Fielding, just as the *Harry Potter* series did for another British author, J.K. Rowling. Fielding now lives in Los Angeles as well as keeping a home in London. She wrote a sequel, *Bridget Jones: The Edge of Reason*, which was published in 1999 — only a few weeks after the manuscript, long overdue, was delivered to the publishers. Given that the film of the original was already being planned at this stage, there are elements of the sequel which creep into the adaptation.

Just as Bridget depends so crucially on her "urban family" of Jude, Shazzer, Tom, and Magda to keep her sane, it is clear that Fielding's own "family" of longstanding friends remain important to her. One of her friends from university was Richard Curtis, later involved in the scripting of the British satirical television sketch show *Not the Nine O' Clock News* (1979–1982) and two successful long-running comedies, *Blackadder* (1983–1989) and *Mr Bean* (1989–1995). He is better known internationally as the screenwriter for *Four Weddings and a Funeral* (1994) and *Notting Hill* (1999) and did, of course, co-script the film adaptation of *Bridget Jones's Diary* (2001). Curtis also co-founded Comic Relief in 1985, a project in which Fielding had been involved, and he merited a warm acknowledgement from Fielding in *Bridget Jones's Diary*.

Again, this makes it tempting to see more of Fielding and her peers in the book than she would like to admit. The issue is not that they might be recognizable as characters in the novel, but that they represent what was, in the 1990s at least, a singularly desirable way of life. They all emerged from the world of the media in London — the heart of "cool Britannia" by the time of the Labour victory in the General Election of 1997. *Bridget Jones's Diary*, set in 1995, is a commentary on the 1990s, but shows the underside of "cool Britannia" in the sense that Bridget aspires to attain the trappings of success—a better job, a boyfriend, more exciting leisure activities—but struggles to control the chaos of her own life. In the decade where the term "lifestyle" took on a whole new meaning, Bridget embodied that quest for "it" (for lifestyle becomes a commodity, a thing to be bought and possessed rather than honed through individual tastes and attitudes); yet her diary reveals that she knows "lifestyle" is all too ephemeral, and the internal contradictions of some of her aspirations becomes only too clear.

BRIDGET JONES'S DIARY

Fielding's second novel was something of a surprise success. It wasn't the first novel to feature the life and loves of a single woman about town, yet it would go on to inspire many an imitator and eventually a new "genre" of its own. There have been confessional women's novels before—the first person voice was in particular a great favorite with feminist writers in the 1970s and 1980s—but Bridget was seen by many to be confessing the shortcomings of a generation, rather than her own particular brand of frailty. In the novel, which spans the year 1995 (given references to the BBC's adaptation of *Pride and Prejudice*), Bridget begins by listing all her New Year's resolutions, then spends the rest of the year breaking them. Much of her social life is directed towards finding a truly "functional relationship" with a man and, if not becoming a "smug married," then at least not remaining a "singleton." Humorously narrated incidents are punctuated by a sense of Bridget's longing for an ideal man and, in the spirit of the romantic tradition, there are two eligible men to choose from.

Fielding, a huge admirer of Jane Austen, takes elements from Austen's novel *Pride and Prejudice* (1813) and uses them to shape her plot. Austen's heroine, Elizabeth Bennet, is one of five daughters born to an impoverished member of the gentry and whose property is entailed to a male heir—therefore his daughters will be disinherited on his death. He has married beneath him into a "trade" family and his wife is unremittingly self-centered; her only real ambition is to marry off her daughters well. The hero, Fitzwilliam Darcy, is an enormously rich and apparently haughty man who sees the Bennet sisters as gauche gold-diggers and persuades his friend not to propose to Lizzy's beloved sister Jane. Meanwhile, Darcy finds himself falling in love with Elizabeth, who has by this time met an old acquaintance of his, Wickham, who convinces her, falsely, that he has been deeply wronged by Darcy. The path to their eventual happiness is therefore made treacherous by a number of significant obstacles: Darcy's pride, Wickham's lies, Darcy's attempt to destroy Lizzy's sister's happiness by discouraging his friend Bingley from proposing, the difference in their family backgrounds and most sensationally, the elopement of Lizzy's 15-year-old sister Lydia with Wickham. As these obstacles start to fall away and Darcy and Lizzy renew their acquaintance, they are both forced to realize their own shortcomings in order to offer the model of the true companionate marriage to the reader.

In *Bridget Jones's Diary* the Darcy/Wickham dynamic is mirrored in the past acquaintanceship of Mark Darcy and Daniel Cleaver; the focal point of family relationships is divided between Bridget's parents and her self-selected "urban family" of friends. Both components of this new postmodern "family" help to prevent Bridget from finding happiness straight away, and Mrs. Jones's flighty self-obsession becomes a modern take on the relentlessly silly Mrs. Bennet. The Wickham/Lydia elopement is supplanted by a diverting sub-plot involving Bridget's mother and the off-puttingly tanned Julio, whose fraudulent schemes are finally uncovered with Darcy's help.

I shall discuss these parallels in more detail in the next chapter;

for many readers this loving pastiche of some of the key elements of Austen's classic work enhanced the pleasure of *Bridget Jones's Diary*. There are, of course, many more who, coming to Austen themselves through film and television adaptations, find much to compare with the 1995 BBC version of *Pride and Prejudice* and perhaps have always imagined Mark Darcy in the image of the actor Colin Firth, who played Darcy in that adaptation. For these readers, Fielding might be seen to be telling timeless truths about love and courtship, whereas another constituency of readers who are less familiar with Austen or heritage movies might be enthralled by the novel's contemporaneity. Fielding has claimed that many women readers recognize themselves in it:

I've talked to women all over the place at book signings—Japan, America, Scandinavia, Spain—and what they most relate to is the massive gap between the way women feel they're expected to be and how they actually are. These are complicated times for women. Bridget is groping through the complexities of dealing with relationships in a morass of shifting roles, and a bombardment of idealised images of modern womanhood. It seems she's not the only one who's confused.

This is one of the more aware remarks from a writer who, although rightly proud of her creation, tends to defend the novel against criticism by insisting that it's "only" supposed to be a comic book. Clearly the novel contains several dimensions: reading it in the light of *Pride and Prejudice* might take you in one direction, whereas luxuriating in its acute observational humor emphasizes other aspects. Feminist-oriented readers might read Fielding's summary above as an interesting take on the way Bridget embodies two conflicting impulses: to value her own aspirations and interests and to reap the benefits of more than thirty years of modern feminism, and yet to want to be swept off her feet by an unreconstructed

Byronic hero. Whatever the conclusions drawn by individual readers, the collective response was to greet the novel as a phenomenon,
as offering something to say about contemporary living that was new
and refreshing.

SOURCES AND INFLUENCES

Fielding's most openly acknowledged influence is, of course, Jane
Austen—a source of inspiration she would return to for the sequel,
using *Persuasion* (1818) instead. When comparisons between Fielding and other writers are made it is not so much her literary impact
that is of concern so much as the cultural impact of *Bridget Jones's
Diary*, its themes and content. In terms of structure, style and tone
the novel has been compared to Sue Townsend's *Adrian Mole*
diaries (1985, 1992, 1993, 1999), Nick Hornby's *Fever Pitch* (1992)
and *High Fidelity* (1995); and, in America, Armistead Maupin's
Tales of the City (1980) and Candace Bushnell's *Sex and the City*
(1996). Clearly, the diary format makes a very literal connection
between Townsend and Fielding's work and in Townsend's most
recent novel, *Adrian Mole: The Cappuccino Years* (1999), Adrian
emerges as a thirty-something underachiever, always on the verge of
some career break and consistently with a higher sense of his own
significance than is apparent in his daily relations with the world.
As with Bridget, the reader negotiates a path between the self constructed by Adrian Mole in his own image and the ways in which
others might perceive him through descriptions of conversations
and incidents in his daily life. Both writers have a clear link with
classics in comic writing like George and Weedon Grossmith's
Diary of a Nobody (1892) which, in charting the exploits of Charles
Pooter, presents a similarly hapless hero in search of recognition of
his erudite and witty soul. All these characters attract us (and make

us laugh) because at heart they are all ordinary and more likely to be beset by the tiniest of domestic tragedies than by the welter of world events.

Hornby's writing was seen to define a new generation of writing by men because it openly debated the qualities of masculinity, and showed young men in crisis because many of the certainties of their fathers' generation had been swept away. *Fever Pitch* and *High Fidelity* share with *Bridget Jones's Diary* the first person narrative voice, and it is a voice that can sometimes feel more intimate and confessional as well as disorienting and suffocating. Hornby, like Fielding, manages to evoke his characters' ordinary world, friendships, and relationships with startling candor, and much of the pleasure of reading his books stems also from recognizing the truth of the observations he makes. Maupin's characters in *Tales of the City* are often more colorful and flamboyant—extraordinary for their uniqueness rather than their ordinariness, perhaps—but the sense of people seeking alternatives to family for solace and coping with the disorientation of the big city is common to both writers.

In the context of the legacy of twentieth century women writers, Fielding can been seen to emerge from a host of writers who have favored the first person, like Sylvia Plath in *The Bell Jar* (1963), and diary format like Doris Lessing in *The Golden Notebook* (1962). *Bridget Jones's Diary* is no *Bell Jar* though, in which Esther Greenwood's descent into mental illness is reflected back on U.S. society of the 1950s and its maintenance of prehistoric models of femininity (even though its colleges were bursting with highly educated women), but millions of readers have seen their own struggle against femininity in Esther, just as many see their ambiguities reflected in Bridget. *Bridget Jones's Diary* has some common ground with Erica Jong's *Fear of Flying* (1973) in its confessional tone, and at the time Jong's novel was published many felt that she told truths about the female condition and the state of gender relations which added fuel to the sexual revolution. Nonetheless, Jong's Isadora wants to be a feminist *and* a femme fatale, whereas for Bridget feminism is strident and unattractive — a popular lament of the nineties woman.

Of course, some of these novels lay significant claim to being "literary." Plath, an acclaimed poet, had also the tragedy of her early suicide to add a mystique to her work, and *The Bell Jar* became one of the defining texts of the modern women's movement along with Betty Friedan's *The Feminine Mystique* (1963). Jong's novel, despite becoming a bestseller and being regarded with suspicion by some in the women's movement, was full of literary references and parody — particularly of the eighteenth century picaresque novel. But the boundary between high and low culture is fragile and often changing; perhaps at the moment Fielding's work would inhabit the "middlebrow" category, even though there are also compelling similarities to the low-brow mass-market romance formula. This in itself is not unusual, as many women writers have embraced the romance narrative either to subvert it or to show its pull on the woman reader, and Fielding's combination of comic narration and whimsical romance proves to be an occasionally unsettling mixture, generating the kind of tensions which have had critics producing widely divergent readings of *Bridget Jones's Diary*.

2

The Novel

It is almost impossible to discuss *Bridget Jones's Diary* simply as a novel. Even before the immensely successful film adaptation was released in 2001, it was one of the most talked about novels of the last decade. No sooner had Fielding's work hit the bestseller list than it seemed that other writers were being marketed as producing their own kind of Bridget Jones: whether Fielding actually generated a new market or simply helped to concretize the most successful factors of an existing one is open to some debate. But for many reasons a hugely diverse constituency of readers feel that there is a link between Bridget and their own realities, or at least that Bridget says something genuinely new about single life. When critics were through with reviewing the novel, they began reviewing the "phenomenon." Some wanted to separate Fielding's comic work of fiction from the monstrosity which they felt had emerged from the germs of the novel but had taken on a life of its own, but it wasn't always easy to separate the Bridget of the novel and the wider claims made about the character. More or less everyone agrees that Fielding is not dealing with profundities here, and some resent the inevitable comparisons with Jane Austen, yet the novel seems to have tapped into numerous anxieties in different clusters of readers and the life of Bridget outside the novel continues, unfettered by any attempts to put her back where she "belongs." I am writing this chapter certain in the knowledge that I, for one, can not smoothly separate the fictional character from the multi-headed beast she has become. I am assuming that many readers are themselves happy to see such boundaries blurred and may even agree with me that the pleasure of the text is in great part its wider referentiality. Observational comedy works because we rapidly make links which themselves conjure up quite disparate responses depending on our age, class and experience; and we make other connections as we read. I hope the reader will agree.

THE "CONFESSIONAL" MODE: TELLING IT LIKE IT IS

The most immediate pleasure in picking up *Bridget Jones's Diary* is its neat and inviting structure. How many people could resist picking up and reading a diary if someone left it lying about? Fictional diaries often capitalize on the thought of such stolen pleasure. Moreover, diaries are not just about the recording of events and occasions but often have a confessional function, and this involves the reader in a voyeuristic relationship with the protagonist. For that reason, even fictional diaries may seem unbearably personal at times and, at their best, might evoke the sense of guilt prompted by reading an actual diary. Diaries promise a closer insight into the "real" person, but the self we find there might be contradictory or elusive. Furthermore, as Bridget notes in the film adaptation, "everyone knows diaries are just full of crap."

Fielding engages us immediately by framing the novel in the neat cycle of one year and the inevitable New Year's resolutions, which themselves offer a telling insight into Bridget's character. We see her as a person who is chaotically aspirational; she is adept at identifying her shortcomings, but rather passive in the face of change. Such a large list of resolutions seems to guarantee failure. The sublime, such as "Give proportion of earnings to charity," is inevitably counterpoised by the ridiculous—"learn to programme video." What is most notable about these resolutions, though, is their ordinariness, their humorous familiarity.

The diary offers the neatest of structures for writer and reader: chapters are named for the twelve months of the year and each episode is framed by the entry for any given date. The book can be read episode by episode or chapter by chapter, which makes it extremely manageable to read in a distracting environment, such as on the train or in a lunch hour—not unlike the glossy magazines beloved of its heroine. It is absorbing and yet leisurely in pace, as the diary combines the eventful with the mundane and Fielding exploits this neatness with flair. Since real diaries are written in a continuing present with clearly no sense at all of how the last entry might read, Fielding's style seems authentic. It is only later in the book when the sub-plots start to converge that the reader senses the firm narrative control of the author. In other ways, Fielding takes the form to the limits by seeming to have Bridget write entries in snatches at the most improbable times. For example, the entries for Tuesday March 21, when she is preparing for her birthday dinner party increasingly challenge our credulity—at the height of very stressful preparations, we are supposed to believe that Bridget sat down to write: "Aargh. Doorbell. Am in bra and pants with wet hair. Pie is all over floor. Suddenly hate the guests" (p. 84). That is part of the humor of the book, which teases the reader by using the seeming discontinuities of the diary form. The way Bridget approaches the writing of the diary and the tone she uses gives the reader the clearest insight we will get into her character. As Alison Case observes in one of the first scholarly articles on the novel, "the fact that Bridget keeps a diary, and keeps it in the way she does, is an important aspect of her character—an indicator of her desire to take control of her life, get some perspective on her more obsessive behaviours, and confide in someone or something."

The first person narrative often throws up twin impulses in the reader: on the one hand we are drawn into a powerful sense of empathy with the narrator; on the other, we feel profoundly distrustful. First person narrators are inherently unreliable. Without the possibilities of balance promised by omniscient third-person narration, or the compensations of having one first person account offset by another (perhaps conflicting) one, we can feel suffocated or implicated in events from which we want to distance ourselves. With a first person narrative, the reader can be tryrannized by the narrator's entirely subjective viewpoint; but then again, third person writing only allows us the *illusion* of a more objective vision of things. A device Fielding uses to avoid the sense of total suffocation is to make the reader feel occasionally superior to Bridget. Bridget sometimes sees without perceiving and the reader quickly puts together clues that she overlooks. At other times, the narrative positions us in a more empathetic relationship to Bridget—such as when she turns up to a "Tarts and Vicars" party only to find that the theme has been dropped.

Any reader might feel empathy with Bridget in the face of her consistent failure to live up to her own ideals, or to make the kind of impression that she wants to at social events—that sense of jarring discomfort is probably universal. But another part of Bridget's success as a character is her particular appeal to a certain group. Bridget and her friends see themselves as "singletons," dogged by the kind of social prejudices that make it imperative for them to support each other. There is a special connection to single, thirty-something females whose lives might be on a similar trajectory. The novel does not, however, solely appeal to "singletons," but in representing a stage of life that people inevitably pass through, there are elements in the novel (particularly in the spirit of the confessional) that might convince readers that they are in some ways encountering themselves. The structure of *Bridget Jones's Diary* sets up an intimacy with the self, given that diaries are conventionally only for the eyes of the writer. First-person narration, through this almost oppressive sense of closeness and through its celebration of subjectivity, encourages the reader to be reflective, and prompts feelings of identification.

Not only can the first-person narrative encourage us to feel superior to Bridget, but there are ways in which it can also allow the reader a certain distance — as when our growing awareness of the chief protagonist's character allows us to recognize things that she is blind to. Most importantly, the reader must register the possibility of Darcy's attraction to Bridget before she does, noting in the process that Bridget is her own worst enemy. While she is rehearsing with her friends the means by which she might finally ensnare her "ideal man," she is being courted by one with whom she makes no effort at all. This sense that we can only watch as Bridget continues to blunder her way through life is exacerbated by the way the book is arranged by key social events (functions, dinner parties) where Bridget almost always comes off as an outsider or makes a gaffe. The dynamic of the plot is served by the necessity of etiquette and polite reserve in such situations — and what Bridget ends up doing and saying is set against what Bridget actually wants to do and say, as confessed to her diary. In a novel that is strong on incident and observations about other people and social relationships, characterization is going to be secondary; in a novel that also aims primarily to be humorous there is also going to be a certain dependency on establishing characters as stock types. These may at times make them seem crudely drawn, but it also helps to make them comprehensible to the reader without long passages of description — which, after all, would be highly incompatible with the type of diary with which we are presented. The romance dimension of the novel does not require detailed characterization either; too many interesting peripheral characters might prove diverting, and even the romantic hero and heroine are generally represented by the ubiquity of their feelings rather than their individuality. Bridget's character is largely developed through the reader's recognition of her responses to shifts in trends and self-help mantras; she is quirky enough, but as a romantic heroine she often represents the frustration and longings of her readers.

SINGLE LIFE

When interviewed on the BBC's *Bookworm* program, Fielding said that "single women today, sort of in their thirties, are perhaps a new type of woman that hasn't really got an identity. And that's all very worrying. Women have said to me: it makes us feel like we're part of a club and we're not the only ones that feel that stupid."

Bridget Jones's Diary highlights a marked social trend — that more and more people are living in single households — and presents the perils of contemporary singleness in a critical light. As with much of the humor in this novel, however, the critique is double-edged, so that single life emerges with a number of contradictory associations. The freedom that single life offers is seen to be compromised by popular wisdoms about the naturalness of coupledom; there is also the association of singleness with loneliness — or worse, social ineptitude or downright unattractiveness. The singles in *Bridget Jones's Diary* never really see their future as self-determined, but are excessively anxious to get themselves paired off. Bridget's fight is against such conventional wisdoms, and she challenges them by exposing the dissatisfaction of the "smug marrieds" she knows;

and yet Bridget's ideal position would be to be partnered but not yet smug. Bridget, frustratingly, is forever identifying such injustices, dissecting them and then endorsing them. This is one paradox that seems to have struck a chord with the readers of the book and it is best summed up by one of her resolutions to not "sulk about having no boyfriend, but develop inner poise and authority and sense of self as woman of substance, complete *without* boyfriend, as best way to obtain boyfriend" (p. 2).

The portrayal of single life as it affects women picks up on a significant theme of the novel: the lives of men and women are seen as moving along quite different trajectories with diverse and even conflicting priorities. Courtship in these circumstances becomes a matter of strategy and subterfuge, where friends are regularly consulted and the wisdoms of diverse self-help and dating manuals ransacked for a grain of truth. This humorous portrayal of courtship as controlled conflict is continued in the sequel *Bridget Jones: The Edge of Reason* when Darcy, overhearing Bridget's conversations with her friends, remarks "It's like war command in the land of gibberish here."

Bridget and her friends rightly identify that, even in the twentieth century, there is a greater stigma attached to being female and single after a certain age: spinsters have always been cast in a less attractive light than bachelors. Whereas the latter have been traditionally seen as carefree, worldly wise and, most importantly, *consciously choosing* to be alone, spinsters are always cast as the poor unfortunates who don't quite qualify as marriage material for any number of reasons. To anticipate my later discussion on the links between Fielding and Austen for a moment, one of the great ironies of Austen's work is that she writes with such authority about family dynamics and romantic attachments while herself having remained single all her life. There are clear social circumstances that could have made a middle or upper-class woman in Austen's day unmarriageable regardless of her own qualities and they would be solely connected to financial buoyancy and family reputation.

The existence of the term "spinster" tells us much about the function of marriage in Austen's day and explains our pleasure in reading about a heroine with outstanding personal qualities who does manage to marry above her station, like Elizabeth Bennet. What Fielding reminds us is that while Bridget, Jude, and Sharon try to redefine their status by inventing the term "singleton," it only serves to throw the enduring stigma attached to this state into even sharper relief. One is reminded of the 1987 film *Fatal Attraction* and the demonization of the successful professional single woman into neurotic psychopath so often copied in later films such as *Single White Female* (1992), and one can only wonder at the audacity of Hollywood in repeatedly portraying single women as inhabiting the borderland of madness. Why in the 1990s should it matter whether one is married or single? What *Bridget Jones's Diary* reminds us, by accident really, is that we are at the mercy of others' opinions and that most of us seek affirmation of our own value from those self-same others. The novel humorously gives us an astute picture of dating and relationship anxiety in the 1990s, and yet the romance element of the novel seems retroactive, reflecting a wish-fulfilment fantasy that love can sweep away all other obstacles.

Although the novel barely touches on modern feminism and its analysis of women's life choices, the stigma of singleness was a recurring subject in feminist literature of the 1970s and 1980s. In *Fear of Flying* (1973), for example, the heroine Isadora Wing notes that "it is heresy to embrace any way of life except as half of a couple. Solitude is un-American . . . a woman is always presumed to be alone as a result of abandonment, not choice. And she is treated that way: as a pariah. There is simply no dignified way for a woman to live alone." Eleven years prior to the publication of Jong's novel, Helen Gurley Brown, who went on to edit the U.S. edition of *Cosmopolitan* from 1965–1997, wrote *Sex and the Single Girl* (1962). In its own way a kind of pioneering self-help manual, Brown's book claims to be "not a study on how to get married but how to stay single — in superlative style." Singleness might have been a treasured state to all those new young women on the career ladder in the sixties at a time when social attitudes were changing fast. But even Brown clearly posits marriage as infinitely preferable and uses her own successful marriage as a draw for the reader. Bridget, as a self-confessed "child of *Cosmopolitan* culture" (p. 59), is perhaps a direct descendent of Helen Gurley Brown and has somehow sidestepped the women's movement on the way. Brown herself has described *Cosmopolitan* as "a bible for young women who want to do better" and even though the relationship of *Cosmo* to organized feminism has always been ambivalent, it has for decades headed the field of women's magazines in championing the image of the independent and successful career woman.

The coining of the term "singleton" does suggest a more positive slant than its predecessor "spinster" — as if it is an identity worth preserving against the welter of "smug married" people. A stage seen traditionally as transitory for most people becomes, at some of the best moments in the novel, a rebel identity with its own language and attitudes, as if in subcultural rejection of the married state in favor of new models of femininity for the professional woman. Yet the novel remains ambiguous about this: after all, the collective fear of the singleton is of perishing "all alone, half-eaten by an Alsatian" (p. 33). The championing of the single life reflects cultural shifts and attitudes, including surveys which suggest that more and more households will have single occupants. Shazzer, the nearest thing to a feminist mouthpiece in the novel, rants:

one in four households are single, most of the royal family are single, the nation's young men have been proved by surveys to be *completely unmarriageable,* and as a result there's a whole generation of single girls like me with their own incomes and homes who have lots of fun and don't need to wash anyone else's socks. (p. 42)

Shazzer here picks up on the oft-cited prediction that a third of all UK households will be occupied by a single individual in twenty years time and reminds her friends of this fact, superficially, as a gesture of resistance to traditional ideas of heterosexual marriage. As is so often the case in this novel, the humor lies in the fact that Sharon's assurance is undercut by her equal desperation to find a functional heterosexual relationship—she gets annoyed with Bridget ringing her up on one occasion "because she had just got in and was about to call 1471 to see if this guy she has been seeing had rung while she was out" (p. 129). This doesn't undercut the fact that the functional "family" which Bridget and her friends forge suggests the possibility of a new set of relations at least as reliable as those of blood ties.

THE *PRIDE AND PREJUDICE* CONNECTION

It is instantly apparent to many readers that the plot and some of the characters of *Bridget Jones's Diary* are to some extent derived from Jane Austen's *Pride and Prejudice.* Only a few pages into the novel, Bridget observes of Mark, "It struck me as pretty ridiculous to be called Mr. Darcy and stand on your own looking snooty at a party. It's like being called Heathcliff and insisting on spending the entire evening in the garden, shouting 'Cathy' and banging your head against a tree" (p. 13). Fielding acknowledges that she "shamelessly stole the plot" of *Pride and Prejudice* on the grounds that "it had been v. well market researched over a number of centuries." Fielding accordingly brings certain themes to the fore in her own work — the sense of timelessness of the true romance narrative set against the obstacles of social life (in both cases, class, social mores, and the different spheres inhabited by men and women give impetus to the story). Austen's writing has received similar homage in the past and a number of writers have written recent sequels to her work, including Joan Aiken's *Mansfield Revisited* (1984) and Emma Tennant's *Pemberley* (1993). Fielding's work should not just be regarded as an appropriation of the *Pride and Prejudice* plot: it also shows a keen awareness of the uses to which Austen is put today, most particularly through contemporary film and television adaptations of her novels.

Austen is credited with producing one of the perfect romance narratives in *Pride and Prejudice* and the novel is held to be one of the models for the modern Mills & Boon style romance. Although these formula romances are looked upon with disdain by practically everyone but their numerous readers, feminist critics have been fascinated by their enormous popularity and unchanging shape over the decades. Some critics, while acknowledging that the subject-matter of these romances is never radical, concur that a romance plot consolidates narrative interest around the woman. For Tania Modleski, "a great deal of our satisfaction in reading these novels comes, I am convinced, from the elements of a revenge fantasy, from our conviction that the woman is bringing the man to his knees and that all the while he is being so hateful, he is internally grovelling, grovelling, grovelling." Other critics suggest that formulaic romance novels echo women's lived experiences of sensing that men still hold most of the economic and social power, leaving women to their central role in relationships and family life. The heroines of these novels, though usually younger than Bridget, tend to have a rewarding job, their own home, and a social life, but their relationship to the hero is always traditional, even if they put up a little "feminist" resistance in the first place. The heroes they fall for are always dark, tall, a little older, successful, surly, and smouldering with unawakened passion. In the mold of this genre, Fielding's Mark Darcy appears cold and distant towards Bridget, straight away singling him out to the seasoned romance reader as the real hero of the piece, whose repressed passion for the heroine makes him clumsy or aloof in her presence. This aloofness, of course, becomes one more obstacle in the path of true romance and thus sustains the novel until the reader can tell, as Austen put it in *Northanger Abbey* (1818), by the "tell-tale compression of pages . . . that we are all hastening together to perfect felicity."

The romance thread of *Pride and Prejudice* is set in tension with the ways the material realities of each character's circumstances are portrayed. Mr. Bennet, with five daughters, his own estate entailed, and who has himself married beneath his class, can only be on the periphery of the social circle of the likes of Mr. Bingley. In both class and wealth the Bennets are found wanting in a world where even financial advancement through "trade" is frowned upon. Romantic and more practical considerations themselves become fused when Elizabeth's growing regard for Darcy coincides with her trip to Derbyshire and a visit to his imposing home — as she later jokingly remarks to her sister Jane, her love for Darcy must date "from my first seeing his beautiful grounds at Pemberley." Despite the levity of her response to her sister, the acknowledgement to herself of her affection for Darcy occurs at this point, though there is evidence that it springs from his changed attitude to her and his polite reception of her aunt and uncle. As Elizabeth remarks to her aunt, "what is the difference in matrimonial affairs, between the mercenary and the prudent motive? Where does discretion end, and avarice begin?" In *Bridget Jones's Diary* tensions between class and social status are again played out, although as befits a novel of postmodern times, class distinctions themselves are blurred and status is more about profession, location, and aspirations. Darcy's profession as a top human rights lawyer marks him out as wealthier and weightier in status terms than Bridget; Perpetua, her immediate boss at work, fits a more easily parodied type—that of the London Sloane Ranger, moneyed from birth, entirely materialistic, and filled with the kneejerk snobbery of the privileged. Bridget's parents, like Mark's, are part of the suburban bourgeoisie whose lives revolve around Rotary Club and charity events and pairing off their children.

Both of Bridget's potential beaux have a higher professional status than her and so she seems to follow the traditional mold of women seeking social advancement in part, at least, through marriage or a long-term partnership. Because Bridget and her thirty-something friends are portrayed as in pursuit of an increasingly rare species—the available sane man—little is made of the wider qualities such men should possess. In a world of "emotional fuckwits," small gestures (such as Daniel's plying Bridget and her friends with boxes of Milk Tray chocolates and doing the weekend's shopping) add huge value to a relationship. Yet implicitly, of course, money and status do matter now that these women are looking for life partners rather than the temporary frissons of their twenties. This is very much the bourgeois milieu of dinner parties, restaurants, and exhibitions, yet Bridget often seems to inhabit the periphery of this world in her tendency towards social gaucheness, and readers are invited to empathize with her sense of being the outsider at large social functions. Bridget functions as something of a clown on such occasions and this tendency is foregrounded to huge visual effect in the film adaptation. In a certain parallel to *Pride and Prejudice*, it is at Mark Darcy's parents' ruby wedding anniversary, celebrated at his grand Holland Park home, that Mark finally asks Bridget for a date adding, "all the other girls I know are so lacquered over. I don't know anyone else who would fasten a bunny tail to their pants."(p. 237).

Despite the obvious parallels between the function of the central characters in both books and the use of the Wickham sub-plot to feature both the Cleaver romance and Pam Jones's "elopement" with Julio, Fielding does not slavishly stick to Austen's original narrative. Nonetheless, thematically there are a number of echoes—the domestic settings, the constraints of social etiquette, the dynamics of communication between the sexes, a certain eccentricity in the chief characters, and the continued importance of the family. Both plots contain a huge element of wish fulfilment and it is the romance that is gradually foregrounded to suggest the essence of a timeless story played out again and again across the ages, even though one can't help feeling that Bridget's generation might have been able to sort out a better mode of courtship, freed from the shackles of Austen's female contemporaries. Mark Darcy's links to Austen's Darcy are very strong—the pages of hundreds of romantic novels are peppered with variations on this character—yet, wit aside, Bridget is unlike Elizabeth in most ways. If anything, her worst moments of self-regard carry shades of Lydia and Mrs. Bennet, whereas Fielding herself confessed that she drew the character of Mark Darcy with Colin Firth's portrayal of Darcy in her mind.

In the 1990s there was a positive rash of Jane Austen adaptations on film and television, one of the most successful of which was the BBC's adaptation of *Pride and Prejudice*. Colin Firth became an instant heartthrob on the basis of this adaptation, which was seen to update the novel in significant ways—most notably the way the male body was framed and represented. The adaptation included scenes of Darcy in the bath, and, with wet shirt and breeches clinging to his drenched body, having swum the lake at Pemberley. *Bridget Jones's Diary* is set in this same year, and Bridget herself is portrayed as being swept up in "Darcy fever"; in discussion with Jude, she decides that Mr. Darcy is infinitely preferable to Mark Darcy "because he was ruder, but that being imaginary was a disadvantage that could not be overlooked"(p. 247). The sequel,

Bridget Jones: The Edge of Reason, has Shaz, Jude, and Bridget repeatedly watching this version of *Pride and Prejudice* — and particularly the sequence with Darcy in his wet shirt.

The Darcy connection allows the interested reader to look for parallels of characterization, theme, and tone between Austen and Fielding and of course there are many; yet Fielding's novel is also completely intelligible and pleasurable without laboring these comparisons. It is perhaps more a novel which is aimed at busy, urban thirty-somethings whose "high" cultural diet is consumed at one remove — as is the case with the references to BBC adaptation of *Pride and Prejudice*. Despite the protestations of Natasha and Perpetua at the book launch party, Bridget represents those who take their pleasures from multifarious means and can "read" trashy television shows like *Blind Date* in the same way they might engage with "classic" literature.

THE FAMILY, CLASS AND SOCIETY

Just as Elizabeth Bennet marries far beyond her wildest dreams in *Pride and Prejudice*, so Bridget's blossoming romance with Darcy at the end of *Bridget Jones's Diary* involves her recognition that he is a good catch in material and professional terms. In reading any Jane Austen novel we get a very real sense of the suffocating social rules that govern possible romantic liaisons, to the point where it seems impossible for anyone to fall in love contrary to the wishes of their family and near society. Young people are never alone and opportunities for private discourse must be planned strategically — such as at balls and other social gatherings. In 1995, on the face of it, there should be nothing to stop the young singleton from approaching the man of her dreams and simply revealing her feelings, and yet contemporary courtship is presented as similarly hidebound by rules, rituals, and conventions: little wonder that the title of one bestselling self-help manual for women is actually *The Rules* (1995) by Ellen Fein and Sherrie Schneider.

Class is still a significant force in contemporary society, and the key characters in *Bridget Jones's Diary* are manifestly middle-class, constrained by the usual bourgeois conventions of needing to be introduced and knowing about each other's backgrounds, professions, and marital status. However, relations between men and women, though freed from the virtual segregation of Austen's time, are portrayed as being segregated just as effectively—through the characters' forceful convictions that men and women are essentially different in all their motivations: where women love shopping, men love watching sports on television with the curtains drawn; where women want commitment, men want casual liaisons, and so forth. Bridget and her friends very clearly want commitment—not something to be achieved through light flirting and sexual promiscuity. Therefore strategies have to be drawn up and it is implied that men have to be duped into courtship on the promise of something more casual. In *Pride and Prejudice* it is everyone else who perceives that a single man with a fortune "must be in want of a wife"; in Bridget's case, men are perceived actively to deflect romance in just one more instance of "emotional fuckwittage." The term itself is hard to define, but it seems to be used to describe any man in his thirties who tries to embark on a liaison with the clear intent of *avoiding* a functional relationship.

Bridget, as has been noted, is remarkably inept at large or important occasions, and the "rules of engagement" for her mean putting on a façade—the kind of "inner poise" she constantly aspires to. Elizabeth Bennet's family's deficiencies—most importantly the irresponsibility of her father and vulgar acquisitiveness of her mother, are nearly her undoing in the marriage market. Similarly, Bridget is a woman burdened rather than supported by her family ties—the staidly middle-class inhabitants of a Northamptonshire village, whose circle of friends seem unchanged since Bridget was a toddler, the Joneses turn into a dysfunctional family overnight. Pam Jones disguises her affair with Julio as a moment of awakened consciousness of the trials of domestic labor and, trumping Bridget both personally and professionally, lands a job as a daytime television presenter. In some ways, the disintegration of her family helps Bridget practise some of her self-help mantras on someone else for a change and she finds herself temporarily enjoying the role of "parent," neatly establishing her as eminently marriageable.

For the urban singleton, social life is often made up of ties very far removed from those associated with family, and Bridget experiences tensions between her own family and friends. Her close friends provide the understanding and solace to help her make sense of her world while her family symbolizes the pull of tradition where being single is definitely seen as a period of transition between adolescence and marriage. *Bridget Jones's Diary* presents some pertinent questions about the changing nature of relationships where more and more young singles are experiencing the alienation of working and living in huge cities with rapidly shifting populations and fewer opportunities to make friends outside of the workplace. Bridget's friends become an alternative "family," in that they provide the customs and rituals and emotional nurturance which dulls the sense of deep loneliness that she experiences.

The world Bridget Jones inhabits is a "postmodern" one, and Bridget, in common with many of us, is left wondering what that really means. It is probably inadvisable to attempt to tease out an exact definition of "postmodernism" here, and in any case, the references to postmodernism in *Bridget Jones's Diary* reflect the dilution and generalization of the term as it is absorbed into popular parlance. But, at the very least, postmodernism suggests that we live in a civilization which no longer lives by huge philosophical or religious certainties, where truth is inevitably relative and where politics is as much about image and the *bon mot* as it is about policy. Class divisions, national boundaries, and ethnic identities blur and we identify ourselves as part of a global village at the same time as we may have strong localized associations. With email and mobile phone text messages fast becoming the major means of communication, we are people who rarely experience physical boundaries to our contact with the world. Naturally, this affects the nature of our experiences, some of which happen at the virtual level — through our computers, through television news and drama. The boundaries between high and low culture are blurred and Bridget is a good example of such cultural promiscuity. As Darcy comments, she is "clearly a top post-modernist" (p. 101). Bridget may have difficulty remembering members of the shadow cabinet as she bones up for her interview with a television company but, as she swiftly discovers, her talent for embracing trivia more readily prepares her for the challenges of contemporary daytime television. Her knowledge of popular fiction, celebrity gossip, and her love of "trash" television make the perfect combination of qualifications. This is not a straightforward celebration or condemnation of the "dumbing down" of our cultural lives, but a well-observed portrait of some contemporary cultural tensions which show how increasingly dependent we have become on the media for the delineation of our own cultural tastes and social status.

THE CULTURAL SCENE

The novel was published in 1996: an important year in the representation of professional single women. It was the year in which the Spice Girls emerged with their first hit "Wannabe," and the concept of "Girl Power" was born. The use of "girl" rather than "woman" reminds us that this was a band targeted largely at the pre-teen market, and that girl power was about self-assertion and grabbing opportunities — a message more palatable to a constituency of young women who were yet to confront the vicissitudes of the labor market and the politics of modern sexual relationships. Nonetheless, the Spice Girls were young women who achieved enormous material wealth and celebrity by working the worst sexist excesses of the patriarchal music industry to their own ends. They offered a dazzlingly complex and contradictory image of the modern woman, showing that she can achieve real power just so long as she obeys some of the rules of engagement — most crucially that "femininity" must never be sacrificed to power. The "ladette," the foil to the so-called "new lad," became a keyword in British popular culture, fueled mainly by the launch of Channel 4 television's *The Girlie Show* in 1995, but actually coined in the men's magazine *FHM* in 1993. What *The Girlie Show* offered was the promise of an insight into how "girls" really behave and what they talk about when they're together; in reality, it relied on puerile sexual humor and implied that today's liberated women spent their quality time drunkenly talking nonsense to each other in bathrooms. In a perverse way, this became a celebration of the range of choices and freedoms for young single women in the 1990s, and single lifestyles were central to televisual representations of youth, from *Friends* to the British show *This Life*, which portrayed the darker side of the lives of young professionals sharing a house. (Interestingly, the plots of both of these series reflect a deep ambivalence about the transit from single life to marriage.)

Women in the 1990s were able to find some powerful role models in the worlds of politics, commerce, and entertainment, yet representations of women in popular culture still seemed to lag behind. The hottest "babe" of 1996 was simply a computer animated creation — Lara Croft. *Bridget Jones* entered the cultural scene amid such contradictions—its intimate diary style seemed to promise another insight into the secret world of women beyond the toilet talk of *The Girlie Show*, and the references and locations it used made it unabashedly woman-centered.

One of the novel's greatest strengths is that it draws on a knowledge of the worlds of glossy magazines and self-help manuals. As the plot unfolds, it is clear that this is the baggage that the average woman picks up and internalizes from her early teens onwards. In seeking control over her destiny and being in search of a conventional happy ending—a meaningful relationship—Bridget focuses on self-discipline as the key. Her diary sets out goals for the year in the form of her lengthy list of New Year resolutions, and individual entries describe, more often than not, her failure to attain them. Bridget as a character is comforting and likeable. Readers can sympathize with her failure to live up to her own ideals and, in any case, she finds happiness in spite of this. In this way, the novel seems to set up a tension between our "natural" selves and the selves we would like to be. It may be part of the reassuring feel of the book to imply that we can't change our essential selves, but it is also its most conservative feature.

One of Bridget's skills, however, is to know her own cultural milieu. In one respect she is the perfect consumer who absorbs every new "trend" identified in glossy magazines and color supplements and aspires to them, whether it be Feng Shui or mini breaks. As previously mentioned, part of her appeal lies in her being an indiscriminate consumer of culture, high or low, without really sustaining a sense of any distinction between them. To study *Bridget Jones's Diary* is to study the increasingly vapid materialism of our daily lives. Bridget and her friends are aware of the language of empowerment inherited from feminism, but they have to confront more deeply entrenched values about gender and relationships which lag behind the progressivism which their material successes seem to promise. It is in this embracing of inherited ideas of gender difference that the book seems reactionary: in the wake of such entrenched beliefs, these women give up and celebrate difference in style — women are seen as the gatekeepers of relationships, the ones that give them meaning.

Bridget is not just looking for true romance through Austen-tinted spectacles, she is looking for a package which seems valuable in the only currency of the postmodern age — hard currency. Wine, chocolates, cigarettes, and hotel trips are all depicted either as a category (Chardonnay, mini-breaks) or as an actual brand (Milk Tray, Silk Cut) which acts as shorthand for the kind of "lifestyle" Bridget leads. The term "lifestyle" itself has shifted meaning from suggesting the individual's way of life to becoming a commodity one can tap into by buying the right accessories and knowing about the correct labels and brands. This is part of the strength of the novel — it uses observational humor to identify painfully current cultural fads which readers will feel implicated in and (through the process of identifying them as fads) superior to.

POSTFEMINISM AND SELF-HELP

Whereas bestsellers such as *Fear of Flying* might be seen as feminist self-help manuals, which through fictional means exhorted women to put themselves first and follow their own dreams uncompromised by the needs of men, the bestselling self-help manuals which Bridget reads encourage her to remodel herself in the image of what men might desire. If, by dint of this, Bridget Jones inhabits a "post-feminist" world, then the term suggests a world that has forgotten feminism rather than a world that has achieved feminism's aims and moved forward from there. It is interesting that while a younger generation of feminists such as Naomi Wolf found old-style feminism stultifying, even a little bit threatening, because they felt it contained at its heart standards of behavior that were too hard to live up to, Bridget's peers turn to manuals as if to find a code of behavior that explains their own sense of failure and gives a means of overcoming it. Katie Roiphe, writing about one of the co-authors of *The Rules*, Ellen Fein, in the *Guardian*, locates a familiar plot at the heart of some of these manuals:

Buried in *The Rules* is the faintest hint of a Jane Austen plot: the man who pursues and the woman who is pursued, the unspoken, delicate, romantic game that unfolds between them. What *The Rules* offers, in its clumsy, excruciating way, is a path back to that mystery, that loveliness and ease. It promises women not just that they will get married, but that they will be in the traditional position of being chased.

This seems to be a fair summary of the intentions of many self-help manuals; although perhaps Austen's heroines are more concerned with being "caught" in a marriage that is both emotionally fulfilling and materially acceptable, given that the "chase" leaves them utterly at the mercy of men.

Many critics have noted the gap between the autonomous career women who populate "singleton" novels and the rather pathetic romantic idiots they become in their relationships. In this sense, Aminatta Forna's remarks in her essay "Sellout" continue the observation made by Roiphe: "Many successful women therefore aim to be the boss at work but a traditional girlfriend in their relationships or a traditional mother at home. We may have laughed over Bridget Jones, but millions of women bought Helen Fielding's satirical tale because they identified with the professional, educated woman who wept over the boyfriends who picked her up and dumped her." These remarks seem to sum up the essence of "postfeminism" and its key contradiction; while the success of professional women is trumpeted and while women's social independence is celebrated in a blaze of consumerism, intimate hetero-sexual relationships remain unreconstructed, and people have no means of transforming their personal life to match their professional life. If feminism is just a little too "strident" to be of use to Bridget and her singletons, it is because feminism is seen as antagonistic to heterosexual relationships in its call for a transformation in the behavior of men to accommodate women's redefined social roles. Isadora Wing, in *Fear of Flying*, still hadn't found a way to make politics gel with her heterosexual desire for a traditionally "mascu-line" man by the end of the novel, and more than twenty years on, Bridget seems to have given up completely. As I commented in *Overloaded*, "this perception of the incompatibility of feminism with having a meaningful heterosexual relationship has unfortunately been perpetuated beyond reason to its current status as self-evident 'truth.' "

Single life may be portrayed as more treacherous than it has ever been before, but Bridget is aware that the "smug marrieds" have their share of troubles. In one of the few moments where the whimsical humor of the novel slides into acute social observation, Bridget muses about the irony that both she and her married friend Magda are dissatisfied with their lot:

Talk about grass is always bloody greener. The number of times I've slumped, depressed, thinking how useless I am and that I spend every Saturday night getting blind drunk and moaning to Jude and Shazzer or Tom about not having a boyfriend; I struggle to make ends meet and am ridiculed as an unmarried freak, whereas Magda lives in a big house with eight different kinds of pasta in jars, and gets to go shopping all day. And yet here she is so beaten, miserable and unconfident and telling me I'm lucky . . . (p. 132)

By the standards of previous generations of women, Bridget *is* lucky. The fight for equal representation and remuneration in the workplace is by no means won, but there has, as Naomi Wolf would put it, been something of a "genderquake." Although there are only a couple of jokey references to feminist writers Germaine Greer and Susan Faludi, *Bridget Jones's Diary* exudes an awareness of the legacy of feminism on women's lives and Bridget's own life is testimony to that success. What is less easy to account for, as Bridget hints above, is the continuing malaise of women (married and single) who find their own autonomy compromised. What all the female characters know, and what makes Sharon in particular so angry, is that aging women are devalued, and as they desperately try to summon to mind older role models (Susan Sarandon, Joanna Lumley) their awareness of the body fascism of their society is as bleak as their complicity in it.

Some critics of Jane Austen have speculated on the influence the Enlightenment feminist Mary Wollstonecraft might have had on her writing. Certainly, the key female characters in her novels are valued for their ability to reason and their broader accomplishments beyond the strictly feminine. In *Persuasion* in particular there is a model couple in the form of Admiral and Mrs. Croft, whose marriage is based on mutual respect and equality. Fielding, perhaps, has constructed a character whose diary reveals that she has lost confidence in the power of reason to solve her dilemmas and she veers between reason and irrationality much of the time. She has something in common with the more feisty Rosie Richardson from Fielding's first novel, *Cause Celeb*, who notes: "funny how at twenty-five you worry about not being taken seriously and take being a sex object for granted. Later you take being taken seriously for granted, and worry about not being a sex object." Bridget's mother, of course, offers a slightly different take on feminism. Having gone through thirty-five years of conventional married life, she determines to get a career and no longer be a domestic doormat. Her observations on married life offer an insight into the arena which romantic novels always avoid, yet any "feminist" message about finding oneself is undercut for Bridget and the reader by her immediately throwing herself into an affair with Julio.

One of the dilemmas of the book is common to most humor we enjoy in any context—that once we begin to analyze it, we find the source of our laughter rather dubious. Many critics have identified this paradox with *Bridget Jones's Diary*—that its capacity to ring true for a wide constituency of women (and possibly some men) means that we laugh spontaneously at the observations and only later do we wonder more seriously at their implications. Looked at dispassionately, we are witnessing the life of a young woman wracked with chronic body dysmorphia, who believes to some extent that her life is governed by strict "rules" and rituals, particularly when it comes to relationships. Some critics have found themselves thus divided: enjoying the spectacle of Bridget's chaotic life, and yet lamenting the possibility that the life of the average young single woman is entirely self-absorbed and completely devoid of the feminist energies of the previous generation. One critic attempts to exempt Fielding and her work from such direct criticism by attempting to separate the work of fiction itself from the "monster who has escaped from Helen Frankenstein's lab to stomp all over the mental landscape of its age."

Despite Fielding's insistence that *Bridget Jones's Diary* is purely for fun, the searching questions continue about whether this is a postfeminist novel and what that might mean. Perhaps if so many people find themselves identifying with Bridget throughout the narrative, they have a stark image of themselves to confront for all the romance of the ending. In the United States in particular, *Bridget Jones* came at a time when *Ally McBeal* and *Sex and the City* were cult viewing among young women, and questions about the future of feminism were being asked. If Ally McBeal and Carrie Bradshaw (and one could add Ginger Spice, and so on) truly represented the fruits of feminism's travails, one could argue that we are left with an image of women as weak, utterly vain, and self-serving—a throw-back to the ideas that Wollstonecraft was challenging in her own work in the eighteenth century. High profile feminists were also in the limelight at the time of the novel's publication in the United States, not least because iconic feminists such as Gloria Steinem had refused to condemn President Clinton's behavior in his affair with the young White House intern, Monica Lewinsky. Whereas *Bridget Jones's Diary* came as a breath of fresh air to British readers, the Americans had already encountered her more wilful counter-parts in Bushnell's *Sex and the City*, a novel which featured Saman-tha Jones:

We all admired Sam. First of all, it's not that easy to get twenty-five-year-old guys when you're in your early forties. Second, Sam is a New York inspiration. Because if you're a successful single woman in this city, you have two choices: You can beat your head against the wall trying to find a relationship, or you can say "screw it" and just go out and have sex like a man. Thus: Sam.

While Sam might have been an instructive older sister to the likes of Bridget, there are some marked thematic similarities between the two novels. Sam aside, the key female characters in Bushnell's novel are also at an age where they feel ready for commitment but despair at their chances of capturing "Mr Right." Again men and women's emotional lives are seen to be guided by conflicting needs and while the women are all powerful in their careers, they become needy and passive in relationships.

THE BODY

Considering that it would be impossible to get an idea of what Bridget Jones looks like from the novel itself, it is interesting that the narrative remains obsessed with the body and physicality as the chief identity for women, and that the film takes this obsession much further. Fielding perfectly exploits this facet of first person writing: there is absolutely no need to describe the physical details of the central character—indeed, to do so would make the tone of the writing rather odd. In third-person romantic writing, particularly in the formula romance genre, the gap between the heroine's necessary sense of her own plainness and the reader's need to know that she is really rather special is achieved by having the heroine appraise herself in a mirror and by registering the hero's response to her. A common episode will depict his amazement at her transformation as she emerges at a social occasion, stunning in a new dress. In *Bridget Jones's Diary*, Fielding manages to convey the gap between Bridget's and the reader's assessment of her worth by the simple means of charting her weight, at the beginning of each entry. While these entries also convey the intensity (and pointlessness) of Bridget's obsessiveness about her weight, they also indicate that she is more or less a British size 12—therefore slimmer than the national average and certainly not "fat" by any definition except that of Hollywood or the fashion industry.

Bridget's relationship to her weight is as aspirational as wanting to be a movie star and, by those standards, she is indeed "fat." Bridget and her singleton friends have, for the time being, avoided the experience of childbirth where the body seems to take on a monstrous life of its own; yet although they all identify as career women with control over their own destiny, it is as if the only thing they might successfully control is their own bodies through monitoring its intake of calories, cigarettes, alcohol, and fat units. The notion of seeking control in this way takes us dangerously close to the specter of eating disorders and Fielding must have been aware what a thin line she was treading, between the average woman who may obsess about her size in an ongoing manner, and the body dysmorphic whose life revolves around such notions of control. Fielding steps even nearer to the edge when she has Bridget in *The Edge of Reason* weigh up the positives of being incarcerated in a Thai gaol, one of which is that "thighs have really gone down and have probably lost at least half a stone without even trying." Looked at another way, the body is represented as chaotic and in need of policing. Bridget might just about get away with verbal and social gaffes, but neglect of the physical is implied to be unforgivable. There is a rich vein of humor here which Fielding taps productively, and also a telling reflection of our own times — in which bodily perfection in women is consistently valued above all other virtues.

This was no more evident than when, on the imminent release of the film of *Bridget Jones's Diary*, it was deemed important that the public should know that Renée Zellweger was not really as "fat" as the Bridget Jones persona she presents. Her "fatness" (absurd as it seems to use this adjective when describing a woman who has reached a UK size 10/12) was attributed to the success of her method acting, rather than to any lack of discipline. It seems extraordinary that while we like to identify with someone characterized by her vulnerability, she needs to be portrayed by a woman with enormous self-discipline. Bridget in the novel is destined never to reach her ideal self: indeed, at the point she reaches her ideal weight all her friends assume she is ill, and she laments years of wasted dieting. Throughout the novel, although Bridget constantly sets herself goals, we realize that they are never going to be achievable; her attempt to remain an "aloof, unavailable ice-queen" ends, pathetically, with Bridget vomiting after a drunken reunion with Daniel Cleaver.

Fielding, via Bridget, acknowledges that desirable femininity is not in the least bit "natural," but rather something all women have to work at:

Being a woman is worse than being a farmer—there is so much harvesting and crop spraying to be done: legs to be waxed, underarms shaved, eyebrows plucked, feet pumiced, skin exfoliated and moisturised, spots cleansed, roots dyed, eyelashes tinted, nails filed, cellulite massaged, stomach muscles exercised. The whole performance is so highly tuned you only need to neglect it for a few days for the whole thing to go to seed. Sometimes I wonder what I would be like if left to revert to nature—with a full beard and handlebar moustache on each shin. (p. 30)

Glossy magazines, in the business of creating new trends and identifying new beauty problem areas, represent body maintenance as "pampering" oneself, yet Bridget presents the truth—it is very hard work. But the influence of the glossies (which has filtered into the lifestyle pages of broadsheets and prime-time television) is enormous in suggesting that a girl can get nowhere without styling.

What is perhaps more unusual in *Bridget Jones's Diary* is the fact that we get no real sense of the physical appearance of any of the chief characters. In the case of her female friends this might be seen as a positive, since Bridget only values them for their loyalty: the only other thing we know about them is that they are both professional women. It is more unusual to find little physical detail in the description of the romantic hero. Indeed, the only sense of Darcy we get is in the first few pages when Bridget's first impressions are summed up by a sweater—"what had seemed from the back like a harmless navy sweater was actually a V-neck diamond-patterned in shades of yellow and blue—as favoured by the more elderly of the nation's sports reporters" (p. 13). Fielding so often plays on our understanding of the meaning of objects—clothes, consumer goods and so forth—to metonymically stand for the person concerned, or a particular character defect. These reflections on character rarely penetrate beneath a person's clothing and even Bridget's confessions may find us startled to realize that she never seems to experience an emotion or physical sensation directly. The daily rigors of life are glossed over so that (perhaps surprisingly given Bridget's zeal for cataloguing things) we don't know when she gets her period—it isn't even mentioned after her pregnancy scare. Similarly, although sex happens, it always happens off-stage and Bridget seems surprisingly free of anxiety about her sexual performances.

MEN AND MASCULINITY

Bridget's anxieties about relationships and her inability to have them stem largely from her assessment of men as an alien species. The self-help manual, *Men are from Mars, Women are from Venus* sums up this viewpoint, and reflects a popular swing away from the feminist concept of showing gender differences as socially constructed, to a new embracing of "natural" differences. Popular science texts, in common with self-help manuals, seem intent on proving that the essential differences between men and women are unalterable and that the best thing to do is accept them and work within their constraints. The farther one takes this, the more unpalatable it becomes: we end up with recent "findings" which purport to show that rape is "natural" and that having a professional career makes a woman produce more testosterone. Bridget and her friends, while not going this far, derive some comfort from the idea that some differences between the sexes are unbridgeable and they leap into a sex war which requires little feminist reflection from them. In the world of dating, it seems, all women need to do is separate the heroes from the bastards.

Men largely fall into three categories in *Bridget Jones's Diary*—the hero, the bastard, and the gay friend. Both hero and bastard have to share certain qualities to build up the tensions between them and, sure enough, Cleaver and Darcy are at times aloof, self-centered and willfully insensitive to Bridget's feelings. Both roles call for a fairly traditional mold of masculinity and it is something common to all romance texts that the heroine can have quite a range of identities without disrupting the plot, but the hero must be tall, brooding, and Byronic. Interestingly, the chief protagonists in contemporary popular novels by men are almost never any of these things—for example, Rob in Nick Hornby's *High Fidelity* (1995) hopes that "women are not necessarily interested in long blond hair, cheekbones and height; that sometimes they are looking for shortish dark hair, no cheekbones and width." Yet romantic fiction clings tighter to this particular image of the male than to any other of its narrative effects. It can make the hero particularly two-dimensional, and in the mass-market romance genre he often becomes a throbbing mass of physical responses and very little else. In contrast, the character of the bastard has to have some credibility and depth to be desired by the heroine in the first place. The bastard carries the bulk of the plot in the first half of the novel because it creates the best initial obstacle to hero and heroine, and because bastards are interesting in the range one can give the character, as opposed to the growing benignity of the hero. Even if Fielding herself had concluded before the birth of Bridget that, "The Bastard's rightful habitat is the imagination, the past remembered or the future projected. Only a twerp would end up with one," Bridget very nearly does end up with "gorgeous, messy, sexy, exciting, hilarious Daniel" (p. 298) and the ambiguity about Cleaver's role is developed in the film adaptation, where Hugh Grant's portrayal relishes Daniel's sexual attractiveness.

Bridget's father Colin is an interesting amalgam of hero and bastard. To Bridget he is a hero by default, being her father, benign, and more or less passive; to her mother in her "suddenly single" state, he is the cause of her dissatisfaction, the unthinking patriarch who has taken her housewifely roles for granted throughout their married life. Unlike the lively, fraught, and conflictual relationship Bridget enjoys with her mother, her father is seen as benign because he is distanced from the action of the novel as a whole. In fact, Colin Jones could be seen as a model for all the "emotional fuck-wits" that Shazzer denounces—he is cowardly and dysfunctional and helpless in the face of the breakup of his marriage because he has left the maintenance of their relationship to his wife. His stereo-typical British reserve (masterfully portrayed by Jim Broadbent in the film) is counterpoised by the equally stereotypical latin lover Julio who emerges as a dashing anti-hero in the novel's denoue-ment. As Bridget notes, "every time I've met Julio he has been clean and coiffed beyond all sense and carrying a gentleman's handbag. Now he was wild, drunk, unkempt and, frankly, just the type I fall for" (p. 302).

Tom, the only gay character in the novel, takes up the role as Bridget's only significant male friend. A self-confessed "hag fag," who "has a theory that homosexuals and single women in their thirties have natural bonding: both being accustomed to disappoint-ing their parents and being treated as freaks by society" (p. 27), Tom is essentially feminized in his role as confidant to Bridget, Jude and Shazzer. In a novel that restricts itself mainly to the surfaces of things, Tom's gayness simply marks him out as miraculously free from the main sins of masculinity. His identity does nothing to unseat the very narrow view of maleness offered in the novel, and beyond the humor of creating a character who is an instantly rec-ognizable "type," his one-dimensional character uncomfortably sug-gests that gay men are simply "effeminate," that their concerns and emotions are identical to those of women.

I have tried to cover the main themes of *Bridget Jones's Diary* to show that its use of irony and observational humor make it a novel which prides itself on its superficiality as a means of exposing the consequences of an acute obsession with the surfaces of things. Given the lack of character development in the novel, it is interesting that readers have felt such a closeness to Bridget, and this is a tribute to Fielding's economical use of well-chosen objects or ideas to represent a type of person. Bridget's disarming frankness in some areas can make us wince with embarrassment, but her relationships (particularly with her parents, perhaps) are broad enough to prompt feelings of empathy in a range of readers. The novel is relentlessly plot-driven as Bridget herself builds up the tension before social occasions often only to fall flat when they happen. The beginning and ending also have a neat symmetry about them, providing a sense of comfort and security. Bridget *is* wanted, despite her imperfections, and the Boxing Day entry to her diary—the last—is stripped of any epigraphic weight and calorie updates. Bridget, in a rare moment of profundity, declares that she has "finally realized the secret of happiness with men" and unlike Elizabeth Bennet, ironically finds wisdom in the counsel of her mother.

I have not devoted a section of this chapter to Bridget herself because the effects of her characterization permeate every other section, and the Frankenstein's monster she was to become is very much the subject of subsequent chapters. It may however be useful to pause here to remind ourselves that for all her excruciating social ineptitude, her inability to judge the right moment, there is another Bridget who is the key to the runaway success of the novel. Bridget's accounts of her hapless excursions into the urban undergrowth in search of a man are written with wit, acuity, and redoubtable comic timing. Perhaps more than the Bridget whose frailties and anxieties we recognize so readily, we warm to the Bridget whose understanding of the chaotic world around her is unfailingly provocative and entertaining.

3

The Novel's Reception

By the time *Bridget Jones's Diary* reached the paperback market it was already guaranteed to become a bestseller. It had the initial draw of those established fans who enjoyed the newspaper columns and might be engaged by a version that had a clearer sense of direction and plot. The book was also different enough to catch the eyes of those critics who might otherwise have readily dismissed the book as another middlebrow romance aimed at a clearly identified constituency of readers. Its previous newspaper existence guaranteed Fielding a wider audience in any case, and the British edition contrasts with later works of "chick-lit." There is no dayglo cover, and although there is the almost statutory picture of a woman, the head and shoulders image is indistinct and sepia tinted: apart from discerning that this is a young, perhaps glamorous woman, it is impossible to detect her hair color or features in any detail.

One of the first obstacles confronting critics was to determine whether it was worthy of "serious" attention at all. Yet this was a novel that threw up ideas and themes easily. The sheer hopelessness of Bridget at times begs a feminist critique of her vulnerabilities and unreconstructed longing for a Darcy figure in her life; and yet her understanding of the world she inhabits summons the *zeitgeist*, suggesting deeper possibilities under the surface humor.

"IT'S ALL ABOUT ME!"

For Robert Yates writing in the *Observer* "The writer has been largely forgotten. Or rather the writer and character have elided." The same could be said of the *reader* and the character. Although the narrative tone sets an ironic distance between character and reader, for many, the attraction seems to be the lack of distance between the fiction and their own experience. The pull of Bridget for many seems to be that she tortures herself with diets, self-help relationship advice, and finds herself constantly wanting; yet at the same time she seems to be aware that these obsessions *are* obsessions and trap her in a vicious cycle of perceived inadequacy and self-loathing.

A number of critics have addressed the "that's me!" response expressed by so many readers and some affirm that this is part of the book's strength. Libby Brooks in *Red Pepper* comments that, "the soaraway success of the first volume of diaries stemmed from its recognition factor. It appealed to the white, middle class, urbanites who reaped the benefit of liberation politics." This suggests that these self-same urbanites in some way resent their "liberation"; that challenging of old identities has necessitated experimentation with the new, but somewhere along the way they have lost their sense of direction. They are busily trying to create new social relationships in the face of the possible collapse of the old order of things — and this in an environment of new prosperity for women. Brooks continues that "it's so much more comforting to believe it's all about calories than to suggest it's a marker of genuine change in our emotional and political landscape," suggesting that, whether we like it or not, this book flags up modern social trends which mark a real shift in relationships anticipated by past generations, but now becoming a reality. From this perspective, *Bridget Jones's Diary* is instructive beyond the generation to whom it might obviously appeal; but even if it does have its finger on the pulse of a certain segment of the population (Brooks rightly reminds us that this segment would be largely white and middle-class), it is also replete with wish-fulfillment fantasies.

Rowan Pelling (editor of the *Erotic Review*), implies that the recognition response lies in an unsophisticated reading of the book, arguing that Fielding "had written a satire—not a template for modern womanhood." For this reason, she believes it is a "dangerous book" causing women to have expectations of men and relationships which are out of kilter with reality as they embrace the self-help logic of relationship success, rather than bothering to get to know people on their own terms. However, readers' responses on websites are overwhelmingly positive, and emphasize that they do identify with Bridget Jones. Whether they see themselves as dangerously duped into a rose-tinted view of romance I doubt: what many seem to find solace in is in recognizing the dilemmas in which Bridget finds herself, and her own ambiguity about attempting to "play the game" and get her man or sit around lamenting male "fuckwittage" with her friends. Inevitably other readers, coming to the novel through the hype, are disappointed and underwhelmed, finding themselves either simply annoyed by Bridget's self-obsession or regarding the plot as a thinly disguised trashy romance.

Andi Zeisler from *Bitch* magazine laments the fact that "no pop cultural mention of either women or singlehood can pass without trotting out [Bridget Jones's] booze-swilling ass as evidence that we're all self-flagellating, thigh- and marriage-obsessed neurotics." Here she rejects the common assumption that "singleton" women necessarily come from the same mold as Bridget; since the growing number of single women is a demographic fact, it is understandable that many would find the "Bridget Jones" shorthand tag limiting and insulting, not least because it underplays professional and other successes in favor of foregrounding constant emotional turmoil. Looked at in this light, the term "singleton," far from casting away the negative connotations of spinster, might be constructing a new more insidious creature who acts to confirm the myth that while the single life may be freer and rewarding for women in a prosperous and liberal age, in the long term it is a destructive and pitiful state. As Zeisler continues, "We're tapping a well of long-extant stereotypes, fears and assumptions about single women and selling them back to ourselves at a bargain price."

WOULD IT TRAVEL?

The novel was published in the United States in 1998, two years after its British debut. There were clearly doubts about how it would sell in the United States, and in particular whether it would be intelligible to a U.S. audience with its largely unfamiliar Anglicisms and references to very British cultural moments and attitudes. As it turned out these features presented no obstacles to the American reading public and neither did the irony—despite the rather offensive British notion that because Americans aren't supposed to understand irony, they wouldn't "get" Fielding. *Bridget Jones's Diary* soon became a bestseller in the United States with very few changes made to the text—one obvious one being the changing of weight from stones to pounds.

American critics pointed out that Candace Bushnell's "Sex and the City" column in the *New York Observer* predates Fielding's column in the *Independent* by a year and therefore might more appropriately be seen as the *ur-text* of what came to be defined as "chick lit." In comparison to Bushnell's novel of the column, the seeming fragility of Bridget's ego irks American critics—who perhaps prefer their heroines to be more predatory and feisty like the characters in *Sex and the City*. The journey of Bushnell's work from column to book to television series follows a close trajectory with Fielding's, but that novel is no diary. The third-person account of the lives of several New York women, with Carrie Bradshaw at the heart of the narrative, is comprised of numerous cameos, where characters meet and intertwine and then move on, as if to mimic the vicissitudes of New York single life. The novel, like Fielding's, is cut into "bite size" chunks as if designed for the busy and distracted reader, but lacks the contrivance of a single romantic plot—the only gesture towards closure being a short epilogue. Fielding's reign over the singletons is also contested by television's *Ally McBeal*, and a number of critics see her as all too similar to Bridget Jones—a little prone to whining, and devoted to seeing herself in the reflection of her latest man's eyes. Coincidentally, *Ally McBeal* crossed the Atlantic in 1998 just as *Bridget Jones's Diary* was being published in the States. The fact that *Ally McBeal* was already cult viewing in the States would profoundly affect the way *Bridget Jones's Diary* was interpreted there—one of the earliest U.S. reviews was in the *New York Times* in May 1998 and took the form of a letter from Ally to Bridget.

The most common shared critique between U.K. and U.S. critics is their concern about a lack of a "political edge" to the book. Many would have welcomed a more challenging sub-text which would expose Bridget's concerns as entirely shallow and willfully ignorant of the contribution of feminism and radical politics to the lifestyle she enjoys. Although many show how Bridget captures the *zeitgeist* in representing today's single woman, most critics want to distance themselves from the idea that Bridget is a recognizable social type, and will instead talk of her as a parody intended to be seen as rather pathetic, while still earning our sympathy.

In contrast, Lisa Habib, reviewing *Bridget Jones's Diary* on CNN interactive on its U.S. publication, affirms the view that we see ourselves reflected in Bridget, saying that "some idealists might see such a woman as a troubling role model, but who are they kidding? I mean, we really do act like that. Bridget Jones is a fair compromise between the 70s-style feminist and the 50s-era debutante—the 90s woman." This statement is pretty hard to unpack but seems to suggest that Bridget represents a shift in female role models with something retro about her—this being the "freedom" to express one's romantic longing while still wanting to hang onto all the material and social gains made by women over the past 30 and more years. For those critics who lament the lack of politics in the novel, the embracing of a passive representation of womanhood rejects feminism and rejoices in Bridget's essentially nostalgic search for a role akin to that of Lizzy Bennet's.

ROMANTIC FROTH?

Germaine Greer is routinely dismissive of *Bridget Jones*, seeing it, with some reason, as "an updated version of the old Mills & Boon scenario"—and this is not meant to be complimentary. In *The Female Eunuch*, Greer had stated that "the only literary form which could outsell romantic trash on the female market is hard-core pornography." There is a more general concern that "chick lit," rather than being a new young genre, is simply a reprisal of some well-worn romantic clichés. Some critics see the work of Fielding and her imitators as evidence that feminism failed to help young women confront the realities of life and they balk at the romance genre underpinnings of the plot.

Whatever one's prejudices about formula romantic fiction, it has to be acknowledged that the formula has endured and has its acknowledged source in *Pride and Prejudice*. The issue for feminists has been to explain why so many women enjoy such a formula — so well-trodden as to be worn out and inevitably conservative in its view of relations between the sexes. It may of course be for the most reactionary reasons, but in the case of Fielding's novel one has to accept that she stretches the formula beyond the usual boundaries of disbelief, making the plot more and more outlandish and cartoonish. This might be seen as a way of undermining the hearts and flowers of the traditional romance. Bridget is a humorous character and is in some senses rightly described by the American critic Catherine Arnst as a "Chaplinesque Everywoman." Arnst finds the Darcy romance plot unnecessary and false because "at the end of the millennium, single women are more likely to rescue themselves than to find a prince in shining armour to do the job for them." The jury is out on whether this is actually the case. It may be that women do nostalgically treasure the romance fantasy even when it is wildly out of kilter with their actual experiences: other critics of romance as a genre have pointed out that it provides the satisfaction of witnessing the hero, at least for once, in a position of supplication to the woman. Set against this view of female dominance in the sphere of romance remains the perplexing question: why do eminently successful women need a man to validate their charms?

POST-FEMINIST WIT?

A few readers have likened the books to the *Adrian Mole* collection of diaries by Sue Townsend. Adrian — another hapless hero, though a little younger than Bridget — provides an interesting point of contrast, being a male character drawn by a female author. Both authors use a sense of the character's vulnerability and fallibility to draw the reader in, but Adrian in *Adrian Mole: The Cappuccino Years* is perhaps feminized in comparison to the formidable Dr. Pandora Braithwaite, his childhood sweetheart and a ruthlessly ambitious Member of Parliament. Both Adrian and Bridget inhabit the same London of the 1990s and their "lives" improbably collide when Adrian encounters the "Bridget Jones" columns in the *Independent*, concluding, "the woman is obsessed with herself!" Mistaking Bridget for a "real" journalist, Adrian composes a letter to her, asking how she got her diaries published. Thus Townsend disingenuously has her long-established fictional diary writer humbly ask Bridget the secret of her success, doubling the irony of the reader's often unconscious conflation of fiction and reality.

Nick Hornby was another popular point of comparison for many reviewers, particularly his works *Fever Pitch* and *High Fidelity* where the protagonists demonstrate specifically masculine attitudes which reaffirm the gulf between male and female social and romantic aspirations, while also showing a much more tender and vulnerable side to men. One of the tensions of our so-called post-feminist society is the way in which such confessions are held to tell us irrevocable truths about the differences between men and women, which they do by reaffirming conventions with which we are so familiar that they are comforting. Although Adrian Mole, Bridget Jones, and Nick Hornby's men are all concerned with the domestic sphere and with the state of their love lives, the male characters do seem to be able to maintain a wider range of interests and identities than Bridget. In contemporary popular fiction there are two sides: "chick lit" (embodied by Fielding, Bushnell, Kathy Lette, and others) and "lad lit," which has its champions in Nick Hornby and Tony Parsons. It is fascinating that over 30 years after feminists questioned the association of women writers attracting only women readers—as if the scope of their work could not reach the mixed audience that male writers are assumed to enjoy—that this position has become more entrenched than ever before.

An early review of the U.K. paperback edition shows intolerance with Bridget and her friends' obsession with the trivial things in life. Champions of the novel will argue that this is part of the superb irony of the book—that it shows a facet of modern life without taking a moral position, beyond Bridget's own wavering conscience that she ought to know a little more about the world outside her immediate milieux. Decca Aitkenhead, writing in the *Guardian*, is astonished that such obsessions are portrayed as something women should celebrate and remarks that "just because this pre-feminist angst is delivered in ballsy prose, it gets passed off as post-feminist wit." She feels that the humor of the novel will soon be passed over so that "the only joke is that Bridget Jones calls herself a feminist." For Minette Marrin who perhaps takes the fiction/experience connection a little too far in her column in the *Daily Telegraph*, "Bridget Jones is just the kind of ghastly neurotic bore I pray my daughter will not grow up to be." Laura Tennant, writing in the *Independent*, asserts that Bridget has to be hopeless, "because she is the scapegoat by which all our sins of low self-esteem and secretly fancying bastards can be atoned." An empowered Bridget would, for her, be an alienating one for the reader. Compare this view to Grace Dent's in the *Observer* who, looking back at the character through the film of the book, states that "Bridget is a text-book example of neurosis, a 118-minute advert for 'getting a bloody grip'." As Katherine Viner notes in the *Guardian*, Bridget Jones is a popular prototype for single women because "it's a lot easier to think that being female and single is about counting calories and flirting by email than thinking that there might be a genuine political reason for it." She makes the point that women who have enjoyed the fruits of professional recognition are likely to want to make their courtship choices very carefully: what woman would want to give up her freedom of self-determination for anything less than a man who will share the domestic and childcare chores?

HIGH, LOW OR MIDDLE BROW?

Francis Gilbert in the *New Statesman* dubs this genre of fiction "thinnist" because of the heroines' shared concerns with weight and examines how the genre has been vilified by some feminists and critics alike in favor of more "highbrow" literature. He agrees that its appeal to a new generation of women readers replaces the once favored Mills & Boon romances: "chick lit" combines the fantasy romance thread of the narrative with an acknowledgement of the realities of young women's lives. They are unlikely to have anything in common with the feisty but virginal heroines of mass-market romance, but may, rather, have lived a happily single life with friends and past lovers in abundance and with an important professional identity to boot. While celebrating the bald love of the trivial in such work, Gilbert finds a deeper meaning suggesting that "when the reader puts these small but authentic details together, a larger, more terrifying picture is formed of a person at war with herself." This, of course, is one of the cruxes of the novel and accurately explains its power to prompt discussion, make people angry, and eventually generate a phenomenon with a life of its own. Everyone can see Bridget's war with herself; some choose to look to the social and ideological forces that might have helped make her that way, whereas others find that her character projects an unpleasantly passive and depoliticized image of womanhood. Both readings have some validity, and for Francis Gilbert, Fielding is skillful in combining realist detail with outlandish imagery with the power to "turn the tragedy of modern consumer society—the truth that materially we have everything we ever wanted but suffer even more than before — into an absurdist comedy: an impossible search for a myth-ical male hero."

The legacy Fielding owes to the tradition of romantic writing may be obvious, but we should not forget that some writers deliber-ately wrote against the grain of the romance, whether it was Erica Jong (who had her heroines confront the reasons why they only saw themselves in relation to men) or the "sex and shopping" novelists of the 1980s — Shirley Conran, Jackie Collins — where quests for self-realization were made through sexual conquest and experimen-tation. In the name of "post-feminism" we are confronted with texts that don't want to deal with feminist ideas at all. *Bridget Jones* may be all too comforting to those who want to return to the "good" old days of sex war.

Just as some critics felt that Nick Hornby's *Fever Pitch* should be read by women so that they would understand and perhaps pity men, so *Bridget Jones's Diary* is regarded as a must-read for men by many readers posting their own reviews on the web. This implies that the novel, for these readers, tells the "truth" about women in some ways; a surprising claim when one pauses to consider the details of most women's lives that it chooses to leave out. In some cases, the consequences could be serious — for example, if Bridget's delight in receiving sexually charged emails from Daniel Cleaver was interpreted as something all women really enjoyed at work. I mention this example to underline that the elements of realism in the novel have to be set against the humor that the detailed obser-vations serve. This is not a novel which throws up issues in order to debate or resolve them, and we should review why so many of these "truths" hit home. Yet the fact remains that many readers find the novel unnervingly accurate. One reader succinctly describes the act of reading the book as "like trying on a swimsuit in a dressing room filled with fluorescent lighting — far too honest for comfort." An-other reader on *amazon.com* calls it "the best self help book you can invest in," suggesting that this confrontation with the "truth" is therapeutic as well as funny. These readers who volunteer their own reviews on the web are, not surprisingly, Fielding's staunchest defenders from wider criticisms of any perceived shortcomings. For these apologists, most criticisms stem from those who just don't "get" the novel.

4

The Novel's Performance

By August 1997, the paperback edition of *Bridget Jones's Diary* had reached number one in the U.K. bestseller lists shortly after its appearance. It was one of the most popular paperbacks of the year — only outsold in the Christmas rush by Paul Wilson's *Little Book of Calm*. In the *Observer* top twenty paperbacks listing, *Bridget Jones's Diary* stayed at the top for fourteen weeks from August 17, 1997, to be dethroned by Terry Pratchett's *Hogfather* in November for just one week, and then retaking the top spot for a further eleven weeks. By the end of August 1997, John Gray's *Men are from Mars, Women are from Venus* had crept from number thirty in the *Observer* listing to number 19 and it more or less stayed in the top twenty until November 1997; it re-emerged in mid January 1998, reaching as high as number five in the following three months. It is intriguing to wonder whether a little indirect product placement in *Bridget Jones's Diary* helped its reentry into the top sellers.

By 2001, Fielding's novel had sold about two million copies in the UK and in excess of eight million copies worldwide. It has now been translated into at least 33 languages and is a global phenomenon. *Bridget Jones's Diary* was published by Viking in the United States in 1998 to great media hype, coinciding with a promotional tour by Fielding herself; it also won book of the year at the British Book awards in 1998. As previously discussed, the book soon became a bestseller in the United States. The book was equally successful in Europe. According to Kate Muir, writing for *The Times* from France in 1998, although *Bridget Jones* sold well in its translation, there were some scathing reviews about this new kind of heroine, some of them focusing on her Anglo-Saxonisms. *Paris Match* is reported to have commented that "We in France prefer to keep quiet about the little miseries of the feminine condition: painful leg waxing, cellulite and bad hangovers."

THE BIRTH OF "SINGLETON" LITERATURE

"Chick lit" is one term that is used to describe the genre which includes *Bridget Jones's Diary*. Although Fielding wasn't the only woman writing about the trials of single life, she became the most internationally famous exponent, and her novel defined the terms on which all other chick lit would be judged. Chick lit is a very 1990s phenomenon: the term "chick" itself—a rather politically incorrect slang term for a woman—had, along with "babe", been reappropriated in the 1990s to supposedly new and ironic connotations. Of course, chick lit inevitably emerges from the legacy of feminism, its writers are a generation of women too young to be in the vanguard of the 1970s, and yet aware enough to have absorbed the cultural impact of *The Female Eunuch* and *Fear of Flying*. Given that most of these authors are about the same age as their heroines (often in their thirties) these women are a part of a generation who felt that feminism did not speak to their needs and hadn't kept apace with its own victories. They perhaps even bought into the idea that it was feminism that had oppressed women by making them lose contact with the pleasures derived from celebrating femininity—dressing up, wearing makeup, and feeling glamorous. There was a significant feeling from the late 1980s onwards that feminism might be restricting women's choices, because it was mistakenly regarded as anti-sex and anti-glamour. Women reacted against what they felt was stultifying by using glamour itself as a statement of empowerment. Perhaps some felt feminism had gone too far, creating an inevitable sense of crisis in relationships between men and women. By the 1990s, many women had dispensed with the aphorisms of feminism as too strident and combative, had toned down their power-dressed silhouettes of the 1980s and sought to get in touch with their "essential" femininity. Bridget and her friends feel that "there is nothing so unattractive to a man as strident feminism" (p. 20). Self-help manuals such as *Men are from Mars, Women are from Venus* confirmed a popular consciousness that the sexes were intrinsically different and failed to communicate because they didn't trouble to understand each other's differences—never more so than in the field of personal relationships.

"Chick lit" underscores this concept of emotional separatism, and is marketed as appealing primarily to women (with the understanding that men might read the novels in order to better understand women) in a new form of literary separatism. The central characters are usually chaotic but sparky single women who know their own shortcomings and find that they get in the way of the perfect relationship. Emma Brockes' comparison of some British chick lit authors in the *Guardian* shows the potential of the formula as used by these post-Bridget writers, and the popularity of the fictional diary form used by so many of them. It is not difficult to understand why these writers are constantly compared to their central characters, since they are more often than not of a similar age, marital status, and profession and they only concern themselves with drawing characters from a background similar to the heroine's. The majority seem to be journalists or in the media, but regardless of their profession, the focus is always on the developing love interest and the fact that their successful professional lives are meaningless without the presence of a man. This demonstrates what a rich vein Fielding tapped when she created Bridget Jones — a combination of ordinariness with a smattering of the glamour which still seems to be attached to any job working in the media. Joan Smith in the *Guardian* has also noted the number of authors who seem to depict romantic heroines that reflect their own background and asks whether women writers of popular fiction are destined to write only about their own experiences. Obviously, this gives the characters the credibility which makes them so readily identifiable to their readers, but it also encourages detractors to see them as of no literary worth at all — as if they are simply confessional outpourings compressed on to the page. This criticism has regularly been leveled at women's poetry and prose fiction, and is often used to imply that women rarely achieve the standing of great writers. Despite such criticisms, this closeness between the author and her characters continues: now that some of these writers are married and have children, confessional books about babies and motherhood are appearing. Perhaps chick lit authors and their target readers will simply grow old together.

If *Bridget Jones's Diary* solidified this genre, prompting critics to label it after women's films (chick flicks) that are also less likely to receive critical acclaim, then Fielding's phenomenal success with the formula suggested that the trend would, at some point, reach saturation point. Jane Green, author of *Mr. Maybe* and *Jemima J.* among others, told the *Guardian*, "I'm sick of first-person narration, and practically all chick lit is written that way. It's very easy, in the first person, to just splurge out the contents of your head on to the page. Third person is a challenge: you have to be more controlled and structured in your writing to be able to handle viewpoint and perspective properly." Green here confirms the worst prejudices about this kind of writing—that it requires no literary skill at all. Jennie Bristow, looking at novels by Lisa Jewell, Jane Green, Jenny Colgan, and Louise Bagshawe in the *New Statesman*, feels that "these books appeal to frustrated university-educated professionals who know there is more to life than finding a man, but are struggling to see what that 'more' might be." This is a tantalizing statement which suggests a level of dissatisfaction with life, common to feminists, but a failure to account for what makes women dissatisfied, and it explains why the harshest critics of chick lit are irritated by the whining tone the narrative sometimes adopts. Although on the face of it the source of these characters' ills is attributed to their lack of a functional partner, in truth their malaise seems much deeper than that.

Chick lit has its filmic parallels in chick flicks and these include romantic comedies and adaptations of classic literature, such as Jane Austen novels. There is also "chick" television in the form of *Ally McBeal* and *Sex and the City* where momentum is maintained over a number of series by the failure of the key female characters to maintain meaningful relationships with men. The whole oeuvre, taken collectively, clearly fills a niche for women viewers—whether it stems from the indulgence in romantic fantasy narratives where the ordinary girl gets the prize catch or, more worryingly, whether a whole generation is reflecting upon what Betty Friedan called "the problem that has no name" (women's sense of lack of identity, confidence, or sense of purpose) in a post-feminist vacuum.

The novelist Beryl Bainbridge, who dismissed chick lit as "froth", reaffirms the existence of an unbreachable divide between popular fiction and high art, implying that only high art can achieve profundity, while the popular remains resolutely vacuous and empty of content. Another literary writer, Jeanette Winterson, was moved to defend chick lit, suggesting that there is room for both the popular and the literary — at the 2001 Edinburgh Book Festival she was reported to have said that she loved *Bridget Jones's Diary*. In one sense, Helen Fielding might agree with Bainbridge's account of such fiction, in that she has deflected any criticisms of its anti-feminism, or assertions that it presents a dumbed-down account of contemporary young women's lives, by reiterating that the book was only intended to be humorous. However, regardless of Fielding's intentions, or Bainbridge's preconceptions about chick lit and popular fiction as a whole, the book sparked off debates that stretched way beyond the parameters of the original novel. Readers are a notoriously perverse and unpredictable group and, just as they may choose to laugh at something intended to be profound, so they may seek truths in something intended for fun.

Bainbridge's comments caused a small stir in the British media in late 2001, prompting a number of articles considering her dismissal of chick lit and some of them leaping to its defense. Jenny Colgan, author of *Amanda's Wedding*, makes the point that for younger women there was little fiction that reflected their lives: "Growing up in the 1980s all we had to read if we wanted commercial fiction were thick, shiny, brick novels covered in gold foil, in which women with long blonde hair built up business empires from harsh beginnings using only their extraordinary beauty and occasionally some goldfish. Is it really any wonder we fell on Helen Fielding so desperately?" I agree with Colgan that the bonkbusters of the 1980s seem utterly out of sync with 1990s living (the reference to the goldfish is to a particularly exotic sex act in Shirley Conran's novel, *Lace*), but some of them did at least flirt with the notion that women could find fulfillment without the endorsement of a man. Colgan sees broader opportunities for young women as writers in the 1990s, with less barriers to those from ordinary back-grounds; how far this is true is open to debate but even if these ordinary writers make the grade, Colgan uncritically accepts that a clear line can be drawn between the popular and literary. She prefers to celebrate these authors' achievements in producing good comic literature that people can read without too much concentration in the interstices of their busy urban lives, and in doing so seems to suggest that such writers should be happy to exist at the lower levels of the literary scale.

There is a media fascination for the hordes of chick lit novels currently on the market, coupled with a publishing frenzy to keep banking on the same winning formula. Others see this new phenomenon resulting in less emphasis on literary skill or originality, to the detriment of British fiction as a whole. Grace Bradberry, lamenting the dearth of British writers (one shortlisted versus five north Americans) on the 1999 Orange Prize for women's fiction in *The Times*, cites Lola Young, one of the judges, who suggested that British women's writing had become intensely parochial. Bradberry seems to agree with this view, conceding that "far from wanting role-models and heroines, many of us want to read about women who are more hopeless than ourselves." In contrast she notes that young women writers in the United States and Canada are still writing about more weighty topics such as the holocaust. One is tempted to turn the debate around and ask, if so many readers and writers have turned to this genre, favoring the domestic over the political, might there not be some important reasons for this? Bridget occasionally agonizes about her lack of knowledge of world affairs, but rarely looks outside her own social microcosm: could it be that women in their mid-thirties identify with this because they too feel powerless in the public arena?

BRIDGET JONES ON FILM

The film adaptation of *Bridget Jones's Diary*, released in 2001, capitalized on the immense success of the original novel and its sequel. Produced by the London-based production company Working Title to a budget of £12 million, the film broke all box office records in the UK for a domestic film in its opening weekend by making nearly £7million.

The film is in many senses a homage to the singleton genre and an updated remodeling of the BBC's 1995 *Pride and Prejudice* adaptation. The film is intrinsically linked to that adaptation, and to *Four Weddings and a Funeral* and *Notting Hill*, with both Andrew Davies and Richard Curtis on the scriptwriting team. The casting of Colin Firth as Darcy and Hugh Grant as Daniel Cleaver only further neatens the symmetry. *Four Weddings* and *Notting Hill* gave new energy to the British film industry in the 1990s and became themselves a sub-genre of romantic comedies: films set in Britain with a predominantly British cast and an American leading female. Of course, in *Bridget Jones's Diary* an American actor plays a British character and Hugh Grant breaks away from previous typecasting as the well-bred, but inarticulate and feckless romantic hero to become the anti-hero, but this slight shift in dynamics only serves to make it refreshing and timely.

The casting of an American actor to play the part of Bridget was trumpeted as the most controversial part of the production in British press reports prior to the film's release. Allegedly the search for the right Bridget took two years and the press were keen to suggest that Fielding was unhappy with the eventual choice, although she has never confirmed this. Sharon Maguire, Bridget's long-standing friend and the film's director, says that "I was struck by Renée Zellweger's warmth and vulnerability and the way she exudes an inner irreverence which is just right for Bridget," and her track record as an increasingly respected comic actor made her eminently suitable for the part. Other alleged contenders for the part were Helena Bonham-Carter, Kate Winslet and Minnie Driver and, while one can see how each of these actors would bring a quite distinctive characterization to the part, it is clear that someone less well-known might fit in with the "ordinariness" the actor has to convey. Despite acclaim for Zellweger in *Me, Myself and Irene* (2000) and *Nurse Betty* (2000), she was still a relatively unfamiliar face to most cinemagoers.

Zellweger's preparation for her role became one of the key talking points before the film was released, part of the "revelations" so vital to pre-release hype. Most attention was inevitably paid to her "enormous" weight gain to play the part of Bridget. This method-acting zeal to *become* the character by gaining 17 lbs to get to 9 stone 3 lb is reminiscent of Robert de Niro's portrayal of Jake La Motta in *Raging Bull* (1980); it also extends to her commitment to getting the English accent absolutely right as well as getting some experience of working in a publisher's office by working at Picador (the British publisher of *Bridget Jones's Diary*) for a couple of weeks. As Shane Watson notes in the *Guardian*, what is most striking about the character of Bridget in the film is that "she is as fat as a puppy," and despite the fact that Zellweger "only cranked herself up to a measly size 10 . . . she looks bigger than everyone else on screen." The sad truth is that ordinariness does not really transfer to the big screen, because everyone else is conforming to Hollywood sizes of thin and thinner.

One of the key ironies of the book is in the reader's acknowledgement that Bridget is not really fat, and the book therefore offers a study in women's skewed relationship to their own bodies. Given that the film has to produce a physical embodiment of Bridget without many hard clues from the novel, any decisions about how she should look are going to affect our interpretation of the film. For Shane Watson, "there's something about the combination of pony-club vowels and pink hamster cheeks that gives Bridge an air of Nice but Dim that she never had in the Diary;" in addition to this, she seems younger than her thirty-something years, portrayed at home clad in pyjamas or hugging a cardigan to her chest. For all of Bridget's gaffes in the novel, we read the occasional maturity of her reflections on events and the acuity of her observations to counterbalance any sense of folly; in the film, she remains childlike rather than savvy.

The film itself capitalizes on the spectacle of its "fat" heroine, and not only is the body of Bridget lovingly pawed by the camera, but most critics find themselves moved to comment on it repeatedly, as does every Zellweger interviewer. As Libby Brooks notes in the *Guardian*, "it is as shocking as it is joyous to watch Bridget's thighs dimple as she hoicks herself into a gargantuan pair of tummy control pants and realise that you have never — not once — seen cellulite on the big screen before." This is true and reminds us that it takes some bravado to fatten up for the big screen; but for all the plaudits, one never feels that the absurdities of our modern fixation with body size are thrown into sharp relief in this movie: instead, it is seen as laudable that Renée Zellweger can successfully slim down to her original size in time for the première. The close-ups of Bridget's body are extraordinarily voyeuristic and we watch with particularly awed fascination as her backside fills the screen as she descends a fireman's pole. Every other costume she wears seems to be cut slightly too tight, such as when she spills out of her bunny costume, the complete antithesis of tone and control. Bridget's bottom ends up taking a leading role in the film, with further close-ups of her bunny tail and, in the finale scene, her satin zebra stripe briefs. Given the addition of a very obvious reference to anal sex with Daniel in the mini-break scene, one can only wonder at this obsession with Bridget's rear. In the novel, Daniel declares that men like a woman with "a bottom they can park a bike in" (p. 159), and the film seems determined to celebrate Bridget's voluptuousness on a grand scale.

The key dimension of a written text that a film can't retain is narrative voice, and so the novel's diary format is replaced by the direct speaking voice of Bridget as a voiceover, accompanied by glimpses of Bridget in the physical act of writing her diary. This shift inevitably affects the way we interpret Bridget's character and motivations—gone are the endless reflections on herself, yet the film tries to retain a sense of the gap between what Bridget intends to do and what she actually does—for example, her resolution to stop flirting with Daniel is counterpoised by a shot of her walking past his office in a transparent blouse. The novel already contains key events—such as the book launch, the smug married dinner party, the ruby wedding celebrations—which can be collapsed into fewer key periods of action in the film, because it is usually found necessary to scale down the action to allow more time to establish relationships and atmosphere. So, for example, the mini-break and "tarts and vicars" party are collapsed into one event. Any film adaptation of a novel needs to be intelligible to those who are fans of the book and those who have never read it. For this reason, the rather long-winded and outlandish Mrs. Jones/Julio subplot is simplified and the latter character metamorphoses into Julian—an aging, over-tanned shopping channel presenter with a very mannered British accent.

It is interesting to go back to the novel and look at what features have been left out and how this can give the film an entirely different "feel". I have already stressed that perhaps the most important of these shifts involves the choices made in the realization of Bridget in physical terms. The novel, in some senses, has the easier option of showing Bridget as obsessed with her figure and general self-improvement and allowing the reader to register that her obsessions are largely unnecessary; the film has to produce one individual to represent Bridget, and there are many ways in which that may not correlate with readers' mental picture of her. Bridget's size in the film creates some interesting and related effects: in all of her plumpness, she represents genuine femininity, witnessed by the number of close-ups of parts of her body, whereas extreme thinness in women is used as a shorthand for mean acquisitive unsisterliness. Natasha, for instance, has a boyish figure and her mannerisms are clipped and bossy to go with it; Daniel's short-lived fiancée is similarly presented as mean by dint of being slim — she is slender, well-groomed, and long-limbed. The key feature of Bridget's character that is taken from the novel is that her "natural" self is infinitely preferable to the self she aspires to. Darcy, in the novel, particularly admires this genuineness, the fact that she isn't "lacquered over," and in the film this is translated into his revelation that he likes her just as she is. The film immediately cuts to her friends' utter astonishment at this statement, and just as this tension between celebrating yourself and seeking self-improvement is played out in the novel, so in the film all Bridget's attempts at self-improvement are seen to be futile.

In order for the romance plot in the film to become quickly intelligible, the tensions between Cleaver and Darcy are foregrounded over Bridget's relationship with her friends. This means that different occasions gain focus — in particular, there are more strong periods of action in the office. This glimpse into Bridget's professional life is an interesting development, given that for many readers the novel implies that Bridget's job simply gets in the way of her leisure time. In the film, the scene in which Bridget quits her job at the publishers (knocking Daniel down a notch, to the collective approval of her workmates) offers something of a *Nine to Five* moment. At the same time, the scene makes Bridget's job seem more meaningful than it does in the novel as well as making her departure something of a quasi-feminist statement.

As befits a fully-fledged "chick flick", the male characters are primarily there to be desired by the audience. Just as Tom finds the fight between Mark and Daniel a "tough one to call," so the film generally seems reluctant to demonize Hugh Grant's Daniel in order to elevate Firth's Mark Darcy. Even the otherwise vile Richard Finch character is played by Neil Pearson, a British actor whose roles in various television series have made him a pinup in the U.K.

Given that accidents always befall Bridget at public events, there is a clear element of slapstick about Zellweger's interpretation which feeds into key scenes such as the fight between Darcy and Cleaver — blown up from being just one rather feeble punch in the novel's sequel, *The Edge of Reason*. Bridget is shown as having a faintly baffled relationship to mundane objects and situations, which emphasizes the slapstick characterization. There is the scene where she holds up her big pants before wriggling into them in preparation for the book launch; when she attempts to cook, she forgets to put the lid on the food processor; a trip to the country on a mini-break with Daniel has her emerging from his sports car with completely matted "big hair". But perhaps the defining moment is the boating scene where Darcy looks on mournfully as Bridget and Daniel cavort in their boats until Daniel falls into the water, only to emerge as a mock-Darcyesque figure in his wet shirt, with a sodden cigarette still hanging detumescently out of his mouth. The Austen links are played for laughs in this way, as when near the end of the film Bridget tells Darcy that he ought to rethink the length of his side-burns: we realize that these sideburns are a direct lift from Firth's character in the *Pride and Prejudice* adaptation and yet we had perhaps not noticed them until this point, because we accepted that "Darcy" was playing Darcy.

Bridget still remains the center of the narrative focus, but our relationship to her has changed. Watching her physically blunder through social occasions without recourse to her witty analysis of the event in question can make her seem a lot less interesting. Because key scenes are conflated, so that the launch party is combined with Bridget and Daniel's first date, Bridget never gets to reject him initially on the grounds of "emotional fuckwittage"; her exchanges with her parents are also pared down so that we hardly see those moments of Bridget being self-sufficient and supportive of other people.

The humor which infuses Fielding's writing is retained by keeping some of her dialogue intact, and by using seasoned comic actors in supporting roles — in particular those who represent the parents' generation, but also in the casting of Sally Phillips as Shazzer. Phillips, a well-known U.K. comedian, plays Shazzer for laughs, further marginalizing the token feminist content of her character in the novel. All the actors play up the caricature side of the "type" they represent — one of the few characters who achieves greater depth in the transfer from fiction to film is Tom, who emerges as a fading pop-star who had a one-hit-wonder in the 1980s.

Many critics have commented on the look of the film, particularly on the characterization of London and Britishness. For Sarah Crompton in the *Daily Telegraph*, Curtis and the producers "have created a fairy-tale England, just as unreal in its own way as Dickensian London — and just as effective in selling an ideal of Britain to cinema-goers abroad." Certainly the film has the feel of *Four Weddings* and *Notting Hill*, with strangely deserted roads, lots of snow, "olde worlde" village scenes and Bridget's improbably spacious flat which seems to be situated somewhere in East London in a building connected to nothing but a railway line. In a way, this fairy tale glamorization of single life in London fits well with the romance thread which runs through the novel and, as the film has to minimalize everything not strictly related to the realization of the romance, the picture postcard scene of Bridget's home village symbolically comes to represent a functional family disrupted by the appearance of Julian. Romance seems to require a rosy landscape to set itself against, and the fact that Darcy and Bridget's final encounter takes place in another strangely deserted London street reminds us that all the romances in formula fiction occur in a vacuum where work and the other petty commitments of life temporarily fall away.

Given the whimsical ending of the film, the photo montage that runs with the final credits strikes an odd chord. One reviewer comments that this leaves you with the feeling that you've just watched a weekly sitcom rather than a feature film, and the stills of Bridget at various points in the film seem to frame her as the ditzy heroine, something like Lucille Ball.

BRIDGET THE ZEITGEIST

Not only did Fielding coin words and phrases that entered daily parlance — such as "singleton" and "smug married," but the Bridget Jones persona became an identifiable character in modern life. For some, there seemed to be a touch of Bridget in all women and therefore the "Bridget Jones effect" was just part of the travails of late twentieth century living, where the popular truism was that there weren't enough marriageable men to go round. Women, accordingly, trod a treacherous path through the "fuckwits" and needed to use strategies worthy of military campaigns. Some commentators have even further extended the idea of the singleton — for example, Elizabeth Jones, writing the editorial in the April 2001 edition of *Marie Claire* suggested that "being a singleton is more a state of mind: the ability to be interested in life, to have a laugh, and to have friends you love like family."

The novel has even found itself in the work of other writers. In Kathy Lette's *Altar Ego* (1998) the heroine finds her best friend, a feminist, not only having an affair with her husband (a human rights lawyer) but also reading *Bridget Jones's Diary*—this becomes a sign that she has "dumbed down" and embraced her femininity in order to get laid, and might suggest that Lette is trying to distinguish between her own novels and those lumped together as chick lit. Internationally, Bridget Jones and Ally McBeal are constantly compared and contrasted to gauge the attitudes of today's young women. Fielding, asked in an interview to offer her view on this possible connection, tartly responded that "Ally McBeal is quite a lot thinner."

By January of 1998 the Bridget Jones phenomenon had been discussed on U.K. network television news programs. The style of *Bridget Jones's Diary*, so often parodied in the reviews of the novel, was infectious and in August 1997 Roland White tried writing a male equivalent in *The Sunday Times*. It was also spoofed in other contexts: in March 1998, the *Guardian* produced a Bridget-style diary column featuring Hillary Clinton agonizing about what to do in the fallout from the Monica Lewinsky scandal. One of the more unusual spin-offs was the "Bridget Jones Night" scheduled on BBC television in the Autumn of 1998. The evening kicked off with advice on how to find the perfect mate, looked at the singles scene, and then showed a documentary on the history of single women in television sitcoms and popular drama.

For some commentators, the real success of *Bridget Jones's Diary* is not in the meaningful debates about single life that it might generate, but in commercial concerns who might profit from it— "the self-centred singleton generates hand-rubbing excitement among marketing executives who realise that the Jones pound, like the pink pound, is disbursed more easily on consumer goods than the one earned by the family provider worried about saving for the mortgage and the school fees," writes Cristina Odone in the *Observer*. For those with a bottomless disposable income there was also the news that in a small way, *Bridget Jones* on film has led to a style shift to emulate Bridget's image. The "young, urban, distressed" look, even her mussed up hair, is apparently being emulated by other celebrities, according to Tim Teeman in *The Times*: "Rough-dry your hair, leaving bits damp. Do a zig-zag parting. Add dulling wax. Let it dry. Let the roots grow through. That's Bridget Jones hair."

Judith Williamson in the *Independent* rightly points out that both the book and the film's adherence to genre is the key to their success. She suggests that:

the achievement of popular culture has been to provide frameworks—precisely through the repeated formulae of genres—for dealing with strong feelings that may not be worked through anywhere else. The fact that they are dealt with entertainingly doesn't mean those feelings are not real: rather, that even painful and disturbing emotions can be explored and safely held by the generic structure itself.

These formulae are certainly resistant to change over the decades, and they are uniquely able to explore the concerns of the present.

5

Further Reading and Discussion Questions

OTHER WORKS BY HELEN FIELDING

Cause Celeb

Cause Celeb, Fielding's first novel and part of a two-book deal she signed with British publishers Picador, was published in 1994 (although not until 2001 in the States). It is also a first-person narrative with a "singleton" heroine at its center, but perhaps even Beryl Bainbridge would be hard-pressed to denounce it as mere "froth." The heroine Rosie Richardson was once, like Bridget, a publicist in a publishing company who becomes an aid worker in a fictional state in Africa that is about to be hit by famine. The novel interweaves her past and present to show how Rosie is escaping her past and her ex-boyfriend—a well-known television presenter. She finds a curious link between the famine-torn state of Nambula and the western celebrities who are prepared to fly out and publicly show their support for the aid work. This link highlights the tensions between the lifestyles and attitudes of wealthy westerners and the values of the Nambulans who are suffering from natural disaster and war. The book is at times uncomfortable reading, as the chapters alternate between aid camp life as supplies dry up and the refugees begin to flock there, and London media parties and functions, where Rosie's relationship with Oliver Marchant is conducted primarily through his assistant.

There are echoes of *Bridget Jones* when Rosie, now in Africa, remembers her own obsession with her body: "What happened to my generation of women? Who doomed us to spending our entire lives wishing we were half a stone lighter? I wasn't anorexic, bulimic, or anything else you could put in a textbook but I still managed to see everything I ate as an indulgence and eating it an act of weakness."

The climax of the novel occurs when Rosie organizes a media campaign (along the lines of Live Aid) to highlight the plight of the Nambulans, and Oliver Marchant is one of the celebrities who flies to Nambula to be confronted by Rosie's new life and a new potential suitor, the doctor Robert O'Rourke. The central romantic narrative thread—with a Byronically smoldering suitor set against an emotionally constipated one—has echoes of *Bridget Jones* and all mainstream romances, but Rosie escapes her self-absorption, and the characters in the aid camp, while still recognizable "types", are drawn with more attention to detail and are set against the roll-call of insufferable celebrities who feature in the London sections of the narrative.

The parts of the novel concerned with celebrity and the media definitely foreshadow the themes and characters of *Bridget Jones's Diary*, but with slightly more of an edge: the ending is ambivalent about aid and its effectiveness, yet at another level it is whimsically optimistic about the future. Rosie lacks confidence and has a degree of body awareness, but is more feisty and decisive than Fielding's next heroine, with a growing political consciousness. In addition,

Rosie's relationship with Oliver takes on a darker edge, whereas although Daniel Cleaver is an "emotional fuckwit" he remains a fairly benign character. Many critics see this novel as stronger than *Bridget Jones's Diary* and, because it emerged on the back of the success of *Bridget Jones's Diary* in the United States, some critics there have actually seen the novel as a logical development. Michelle Goldberg, writing on the Metroactive books site, states that knowing *Cause Celeb* was published first "makes the vapidity of the *Bridget Jones* books perplexing."

Bridget Jones: The Edge of Reason

Apparently Fielding wrote *The Edge of Reason* in a hotel room in Los Angeles after one of her publicity tours, months after the manuscript had been promised to her publishers. She had already embarked on the script for the film version of *Bridget Jones's Diary*, which explains some thematic links the film shares with *The Edge of Reason*.

The novel opens sinisterly with the chapter "Happily ever after" suggesting that Bridget is yet to enter the temple of smug marrieddom, or even a functional relationship with Mark Darcy. Sure enough, the obstacles emerge immediately, from Bridget finding that a steady boyfriend can cause tensions in your social life with your regular friends (especially when Sharon accuses her of turning into a Smug-Going-Out-With-Someone) to Darcy skeptically eavesdropping while Bridget coaches her friends in the manner of a talking self-help manual while their supper disintegrates on the stove. The theme of self-help rhetoric weaves itself closely into the plot, mirroring elements of Jane Austen's *Persuasion*, where Anne Elliot suffers from too much well-meant advice from her friends and nearly never marries her beau Captain Wentworth. For all his scorn about self-help, Darcy seems impressed when Bridget appears able to coach his colleague Giles Benwick through a disintegrating marriage. Meanwhile, Bridget's friends decide that Mark is suffering from "Mentionitis," having met one of their acquaintances, Rebecca, at a party, which to them suggests that he is attracted to her. Self-help references go from sublime to ridiculous when Jude declares that "there's nothing a man finds more attractive than a woman who is in love with him" and has to admit that this is actually a quotation from the Baroness in *The Sound of Music*.

Bridget's professional life takes a surreal turn as the daytime television media is portrayed as surviving on mediocrity or humiliation. Her boss Richard Finch dreams up a scheme where Bridget would try a new profession each week and be incredibly bad at all of them. She tries to break into journalism and the Colin Firth/Darcy references really take off in this sequel, culminating in Bridget's farcical interview with Colin Firth in Rome — which has to be published as a direct transcript because she utterly fails to meet her deadline. Firth has subsequently confirmed that the interview actually took place in Rome with him playing himself and Fielding being Bridget.

The flawed advice of her friends, coupled with Bridget's own misperceptions of herself, threaten to destroy her relationship with Mark as they are pulled apart by misunderstandings. Madga and Jeremy have a stronger role in this novel, with Magda obviously becoming a Mrs. Croft figure — the character in *Persuasion* who represents clear thinking and is an equal partner in her marriage. More children appear in this novel, and Magda at one point leaves hers with Bridget, hinting that Bridget is having to grow up in more ways than one.

A couple of scenes from Austen's *Persuasion* are paralleled in *The Edge of Reason*, and there are a number of parallel characters besides Magda and Bridget who develops traits of Anne Elliot, Austen's oldest unmarried heroine. Giles Benwick mirrors Captain

Benwick, whose fiancée has died, and he develops a strong affection for Anne before finally falling for the flighty Louisa Musgrove. Rebecca (another example of the bad-because-she-is-thin female character) is the Louisa Musgrove figure who injures herself by jumping off the Cobb at Lyme Regis, whereas Rebecca dives into shallow water while trying to flirt with Mark. Bridget, like Anne Elliot, becomes resourceful when the occasion demands, and her role in dealing with Rebecca's accident and Giles's suicide attempt earns her Mark's respect again, just as Anne is reappraised by Captain Wentworth in *Persuasion*. Anne Elliot finally confirms her worth in Wentworth's eyes when she defends women against the accusation that they are fickle in love, saying, "We certainly do not forget you so soon as you forget us. It is, perhaps, our fate rather than our merit. We cannot help ourselves. We live at home, quiet, confined, and our feelings prey upon us." Bridget's version of this speech in *The Edge of Reason* is, "If we love someone it's pretty hard to get them out of our system when they bugger off."

This novel, in common with *Bridget Jones's Diary*, has its share of outlandish subplots and comic situations. It also lapses into farce, fused with a commentary on the events of 1997, notably when the press coverage of Bridget's return from a Thai jail is eclipsed by the death of Diana, Princess of Wales. Fielding captures the mood of national mourning on the edge of hysteria in the scene where Bridget's beautician fails to turn up to work "because of Diana." The title suggests a darkness that the sequel doesn't deliver, and Fielding has said that she thought it up as a jokey response to the comments of an Italian critic who seemed to interpret *Bridget Jones's Diary* in a somewhat existential light. It might be stretching credibility too far to see it as a curious homage to Jean-Paul Sartre's *The Age of Reason*, but the title reminds us that Bridget and her friends have overstepped the mark this time in their gross misreading of Mark Darcy's motivations.

Post Sequel

Lynne Truss, reviewing *The Edge of Reason* in *The Sunday Times*, wonders "how many times can you define the comic zeitgeist?" She argues that what she terms "recognition humour" has superseded wit and satire, but that the *Bridget Jones's Diary*'s formula is rather too old hat to repeat. It is not clear whether Fielding has ruled out another Bridget book, but she has since only produced a slim Bridget spin off, *Bridget Jones's Guide to Life*, for the charity Comic Relief. This includes a classic Bridget-ism — her take on famine: "if in one half of the world people are trying to stop themselves eating food in case they can't fit into their skirts, and in the other half of the world people are trying frantically to find something to eat because if they don't they will die, then it is perfectly obvious that it is not so much complicated as not fair." Bridget's character has moved on from its original birthplace in *Bridget Jones's Diary*, and the true testament to Fielding's success as a novelist is that one can imagine what Bridget might say in numerous situations: indeed, people are seeing Bridget Jones everywhere.

QUESTIONS FOR DISCUSSION

Some of the following questions are closely text-based and some look beyond the novel to contemporary issues. Some of them pick up on issues discussed earlier in this book and give the reader a chance to pause and reflect on their own reading of the novel.

1. Given the intimacy of the diary format, why doesn't Bridget talk about her periods or her sex life in any detail?
2. How did you imagine Bridget Jones physically? What evidence from the novel did you use to construct your idea of Bridget?

3. Do you think the novel succeeds because of the diary structure, or in spite of it?

4. Bridget has a reasonably good job and in the course of the novel moves on to even better prospects; why do we hear nothing significant about her work?

5. For all their plans and stratagems, are Bridget and her friends essentially passive in their own destinies?

6. Is there something depressing in the return of the strong silent hero at the end?

7. Try rewriting/retelling a part of *Bridget Jones's Diary* in the third person and note the effect it has on the shape of the story.

8. Is Bridget's mum the real feminist conscience of the novel?

9. If you were adapting the novel for the screen what would you leave out or emphasize? Who would play Bridget Jones?

10. Fielding is quick to reiterate that the novel was just written for fun. Does this make wider observations about its critique of modern culture irrelevant?

11. Which one of the characters in the novel would be most likely to read *Bridget Jones's Diary*?

BIBLIOGRAPHY

Books by Helen Fielding

Fielding, H. *Cause Celeb*, London: Picador. 1994.
———. *Bridget Jones's Diary*, London: Picador. 1996.
———. *Bridget Jones: The Edge of Reason*, London: Picador. 1999.
———. *Bridget Jones's Guide to Life*, London: Picador. 2001.

Further Reading and Reference

Aitkenhead, D. "Bridget Jones: don't ya just love her?" *Guardian*. 8 August, 1997.

Bradberry, G. "Where have the real heroines gone?" *The Times*, 11 May, 1999.

Bristow, J. "Girls just wanna have fun" *New Statesman*. 24 September 2001, p. 53.

Brockes, E. "The Lit Girls" *Guardian*, 21 July, 2000.

Brooks, L "The joke's on us, girls" *Red Pepper*. December/January 1999. p. 8.

Brooks, L. "No, I'm not Bridget Jones. Not Yet" *Guardian*, 13 April 2001.

Brown, H.G. *Sex and the Single Girl*. New York: Bernard Geiss Associates, 1962.

Bushnell, C. *Sex and the City*. London: Abacus, 1996.

Case, A. "Authenticity, Convention and *Bridget Jones's Diary*. *Narrative*. May 2001, Volume 9.

Colgan, J. "We Know the Difference Between Foie Gras and Hula Hoops, Beryl, But Sometimes We Just Want Hula Hoops". *Guardian*. 24 August, 2001.

Cooke, R. "Beyond Bridget". *Telegraph Magazine*. 7 April 2001.

Crompton, S. "Curtis Land in 10 Steps." *Daily Telegraph*. 7 April 2001.

Davis, A. "Back with a bump". *Guardian*. 17 September 2001.

Dawson, J. "Keeping up with Bridget Jones". *Observer*. 27 August 2000.

Dent, G. "Giving up on the Joneses". *Observer*. 7 April 2001.

Elworthy, C. "Bridget and me". *Guardian*. 4 April 2001.

Fielding, H. "About Men About Women". *Guardian*. 17 July 1994.

Fielding, H. "Me and Ms Jones". *The Sunday Times*. 21 November 1999.

Forma, A. "Sellout." *On the Move: Feminism for a New Generation*. N. Walter ed. London, Virago. 1999.

Gibbons, F. "£7m Bridget Jones keeps up with blockbuster hits". *Guardian*. 18 April 2001.

Gilbert, F. "Why I love Bridget Jones". *New Statesman*. 26 July 1999.

Greer, G. *The Whole Woman*. London: Doubleday. 1999.

Jones, L. "Me, myself & Bridget Jones". *The Sunday Times*. 4 March 2001.

Jong, E. *Fear of Flying*. London: Grafton Books. 1973.

Lambert, A. "Women Behaving Badly". *Prospect* (UK edition). February 2000.

Leadbeater, C. "I needed a woman who was an emotional mess. So I gave birth to Bridget". *Independent*. 5 April 2001.

Lette, K. *Altar Ego*. London: Picador. 1998.

Marie Claire (UK edition). April 2001.

Marrin, M. "The Ranks of Bridget Joneses Are Nothing To Laugh About". *The Daily Telegraph*. 14 April 2001.

Martens, L. *The Diary Novel*. Cambridge: Cambridge University Press. 1985.

McFerran, A. "It's Time I Split Up With Bridget Jones". *Sunday Times*. 1 April 2001.

Modleski, T. *Loving With a Vengeance: Mass-produced Fantasies for Women*. New York: Methuen. 1982.

Muir, K. "Kate Muir's Diary". *The Times*. 20 June 1998.

Odone, C. "Alone with Bridget". *Observer*. 15 April 2001.

O'Sullivan, C. "The good, the bad and the frumpy". *Independent*. 13 April 2001.

O'Toole, L. "Strong, silent. Typecast". *The Times*. 9 April 2001.

Parsons, T. "Bridget's just like Bambi with a fag in her mouth . . . oh, how I adore her". The *Mirror*. 19 April 2001.

Pelling, R. "You've Only Got Yourself to Blame, Bridget Jones . . ." *Daily Mail*. 6 April 2000.

Raven, C. "Why Bridget Does Let Women Down". *Guardian*. 17 April 2001.

Roiphe, K. "Why We All Want a Happy Ending". *Guardian*. 27 March 2001.

Smith, J. "Real Life Writ Large". *Guardian*. 4 May 2000.

Steiner, S. "Twice Shy". *Guardian*. 31 March 2001.

Teeman, T. "Bridget's Singular Style". *The Times*. 9 March 2001.

Tennant, L. "A Flawless Accent, Funny Script and Some Filthy Humour". *Independent*. 5 April 2001.

Thorpe, V. "Helen Fielding: Private diarist (vg)". *Observer*. 8 April 2001

Tonkin, B. "Bridget, A Rampaging Monster Stomping All Over Our Age". *Independent*. 5 April 2001.

Townsend, S. *Adrian Mole: The Cappuccino Years*. Harmondsworth: Penguin. 1999.

Truss, L. "Keeping Up With the Jones". *The Sunday Times*. 21 November 1999.

Viner, K. "The Phenomenon of the Singletons". *Guardian*. 11 September 1997.

Watson, S. "Bad News About the Bridget Jones Film—It's So Last Century". *Guardian*. 6 April 2001.

Whelehan, I. *Overloaded: Popular Culture and the Future of Feminism*. London: The Women's Press 2000.

Williamson, J. "Essays In Uncool". *Independent*. 8 April 2001.

Yates, R. "Helen Fielding: Everywoman's Woman". *Observer*, 31 May 1998.

Useful Websites

Arnst, C. "Single Women In a Hostile World". 7 July 1998. *http://www.businessweek.com/1998/28/b3586044.html*

"Bainbridge Denounces Chick-lit As 'Froth." *Guardian Unlimited*. 23 August 2001: *http://www.books.guardian.co.uk/bookerprize2001/story/0,1090,541335,00.html*

BBC Radio Four: Bookworm, Programme 4 *http://www.bbc.co.uk/education/archive/bookworm/tran4.html*

Goldberg, M. "Cause For Celebration". 2001. *http://ww.metroactive.com/papers/metro/04.12.01/fielding-0115.html*

Habib, L. "Bridget Jones' Is Today's Everywoman, Role Model Or Not, and We Like Her Like That" 1998. *http://www.cnn.com/books/reviews/9807/04/review.bridget.jones.diary/*

Time internet interview with Helen Fielding. *http://www.time.com/time/community/transcripts/chattr061698.html*

Transcript of CNN interview with Helen Gurley Brown aired 18 January 1998. *http://cnn.com/TRANSCRIPTS/9801/18/pin.00.html*

Zahra, T "The Feminism Gap". The American Prospect Online, Issue 42. January-February, 1999. *http://www.prospect.org/archives/42/42zahra.html*

Zeisler, A. "Marketing Miss Right". 1999. *http://www.bitchmagazine.com/archives/12_99missr/miss.html*